LIFE TRAP

FROM CHILD VICTIM TO ADULT VICTIMIZER

A memoir from twenty-eight years as a
prison psychologist studying the causes and
treatment of domestic violence offenders

LINDA NAUTH

Licensed Psychologist

PAGE PUBLISHING, INC.
New York, NY

First originally published by Page Publishing, Inc. 2018

ISBN 978-1-64298-456-9 (Paperback)
ISBN 978-1-64298-457-6 (Digital)

Printed in the United States of America

Homework assignment in domestic violence treatment: Link a childhood memory to an adult attitude problem.

Childhood Memory

I remember vividly when my biological father came to pick up me and my brothers and sisters one weekend. We hadn't seen him in a long time. I was so damn excited about him showing up to take us that I ran outside in the night screaming with joy and happiness. I then jumped in the front seat of his green Ford pick-up. After he got in, he hit me right in my face with his hand because I was loud and making too much noise.

Adult Attitude

No matter what good things come in to my life, I never, ever think it's going to last. I'm either going to lose it, it's going to be taken away, or I'm going to be let down in one way or another.

Happiness isn't a state of being. It's given to you momentarily as a cruel trick by God to remind you how much your life is shit.

Introduction

The room was quiet as Carla shared her story. "We got into an argument, and he began calling me names. He followed me upstairs and slapped me in the back of the head. One week later, he got angry with me because I had burned his bacon. He began calling me names and punched me with both fists in the chest."

At the time, Carla was in the shelter at PAVE (People Against a Violent Environment), a non-profit community organization in Beaver Dam, Wisconsin. I volunteered with PAVE for almost thirty years in several capacities—running the children's group, the women's support group, and as a board member. As a board member, I was basically useless—what did I know about fixing roofs or budgeting for driveway repairs? I was a treatment person.

Facilitating the women's support group was where I met Carla and many women like her. Six to eight women would meet for two hours in the basement of the shelter, sitting around an overly large table stuffed into huge chairs to share their stories and find solace in each other. Carla was afraid that her husband would actually kill her. She left her home and everything she knew because she didn't want to die. It was a matter of her survival. Each woman talked about her trauma, relived, it and were assured that now they were safe.

Carla continued her story. "Later, we got into another argument. We both had been drinking and he was calling me a whore and accusing me of sleeping with one of my old boyfriends. I followed him down to the basement. where he showed me a rope and put it around his neck threatening to hang himself. I started slapping him so he would take off the rope around his neck. And once he did, we went upstairs.

"I told him I was leaving, and he said if I did, he'd kill me and then kill himself. He went into the kitchen and got a knife."

I had heard this scenario before; it was a common theme. I was outraged and felt her emotional pain, but there was always another question nagging in my mind. What was that man thinking? What did he hope to accomplish by physically attacking the woman he said he loved? What was so important about that bacon being perfectly browned that motivated violence? Was this victimizer just mean, or even evil? Or was there something deeper?

My full-time employment, working in the Wisconsin Department of Corrections as a prison psychologist for twenty-eight years, gave me the opportunity to answer my questions. As a clinician and treatment provider working with men convicted of domestic violence, I had access into the mental state of the offender. I asked the *why* questions. Why were you violent? What were you thinking and feeling when you decided to hit your partner? I was a cognitive psychologist with a focus on the offender's motivation, attitudes and beliefs, goals and fears that led to their interpersonal aggression.

I never hesitated to ask these questions of even the most violent convicted felon. I reached out to the part of the offender who entered his relationship with the goal of loving and feeling loved. Violence with an intimate partner is inherently irrational and self-defeating. I offered to help the offender understand why he kept repeating aggression despite the negative consequences. I wanted to figure out together how he could change things. I wanted to help him stop the violence.

My interest in violence began professionally when I completed the requirements for my school psychologist license. In 1978, I began working as an intern school psychologist at the Ethan Allen School for Boys (EAS) in Wales, Wisconsin, one of the two state juvenile institutions in the state correctional system.

As I was completing graduate school, JoAnn Myrick, MS, a very competent and well-respected school psychologist, was charged with introducing special education to the juvenile correctional system. The state was following a federal mandate for all schools to make accommodations for students diagnosed with EEN, Exceptional

Educational Needs. JoAnn hired a team of specialists: three teachers specialized in teaching children with special needs, a speech therapist and three school psychologists. I was brought on as an intern.

Each member of the multidisciplinary team individually assessed the child for intellectual deficits, learning problems, achievement levels, and special needs. Then they would meet as a group to write up a treatment plan called an IEP, an Individualized Educational Plan.

As a team, we were dedicated and productive. JoAnn was a supportive supervisor and who encouraged the team members to achieve at their optimal level of functioning. I felt relaxed and improved my work competencies quickly and effortlessly. My naturally warm therapeutic style was nurtured by JoAnn and seemed to blossom.

After my internship, I was hired as a limited-term employee (LTE) for two years at EAS. The juvenile offenders ranged in age from eleven to seventeen, arrived in prison with extensive histories of aggressive and criminal behavior and hailed from every part of Wisconsin state. The offenders from rural, upstate Wisconsin were mixed with boys from the most violent streets in Milwaukee.

The school was situated in a beautiful wooded area in the Kettle Moraine (state) Forest. The buildings in the sprawled-out campus had previously housed patients at a former tuberculosis sanatorium and now boasted a high-security fence. I was not involved with security or punishment of the inmates. My goal was treatment. And I was overwhelmed by the emotional neediness of the boys.

Despite the history of violence, most of the boys presented as compliant and eager to please. These were the children who had fallen through the cracks in their public schools and now felt like misfits and throwaways. Taken away from their homes and communities, most of the boys I met at EAS were starved for affection. I'd see their faces and posture brighten and strengthen in response to even a small sign of kindness, a smile, some praise, or other evidence of caring from the staff member.

Most of the juvenile offenders exhibited some kind of learning disability. As the school psychologist, I gave an intelligence test, a forty-five- to sixty-minute set of tasks the child had to solve called the Wechsler Intelligence Scale for Children-revised (WISC-R). The child's ability to solve the problems yielded an estimate level of their ability to learn.

In addition to a general intelligence score, the Full Scale IQ (intelligence quotient), the Wechsler test in 1978 also provided a verbal IQ score versus a performance IQ score.

The verbal IQ score measured verbal concept formation, verbal reasoning, and general information, such as "What country is north of the United States?" (Not Michigan, a too common answer.) The similarities subtest asked the child how two objects were alike. Finding similarities is a task of abstract, verbal reasoning.

The second scale, the performance IQ, assessed nonverbal reasoning, like the block design tests, when children were timed as they put together red and white blocks in a pattern according to a displayed model. The subtests assessed visual-spatial reasoning and abstract categorical reasoning using pictures and concept formation.

A learning disability is diagnosed when the verbal and performance scales differs significantly. The student then qualifies for extra attention and individualized educational plans. In the juvenile prison, I found most of the students demonstrated a significantly higher nonverbal score over a verbal IQ level, a pattern common in the delinquent population. The pattern also is indicative of childhood trauma; the children are street smart since they are forced to survive in a hostile environment but experience difficulty learning in a traditional classroom setting.

Many other signs of traumatic childhoods were apparent in these troubled adolescents. I recall one twelve-year-old dashing about, too hyperactive to sit in a chair and pay attention to my questions. He was in a rage and ran down the school hallway with security guards following him. I remember this student, Milo, mostly for the vivid and horrifying nature of his social services reports.

Milo, at age six, was found by city case workers with four other children, his age or younger, in an abandoned inner city apartment with no running water, no food in the refrigerator, and no adults on the premises for days at a time. Reports documented the children running around the apartment poorly clothed, amid battered and torn furniture. There was little hygiene. The children urinated into jars on the floor.

The effects of such extreme neglect are incalculable. According to Dave Ziegler, the executive director of SCAR/Jasper Mountain, an inpatient treatment program based in Oregon that treats some of society's most damaged children, "Neglect appears to be the most pervasive and persistent form of trauma when considering implications with a lifelong trajectory."

In *Traumatic Experience and the Brain: A Handbook for Understanding and Treating Those Traumatized as Children,* Ziegler continued, "Neglect affects every aspect of the developing neurological system. The lack of stimulation can cause atrophy to neurons that are ready at birth to go into service as the child experiences the new world."

Chronic neglect results in an overall smaller brain size and in smaller, less developed brain centers in the areas dedicated to emotional regulation and forming and retrieving verbal and emotional memories.

Traumatized children have smaller corpus callosum, the main neurological pathway integrating the two halves of the brain, linking the emotional right side with the rational and logical left side. A less developed corpus callosum limits the ability of the child in the use of their rational brains to manage their impulses and emotional swings.

Ziegler reported that 60 to 70 percent of children who entered his program over the years were diagnosed as having Attention Deficit Disorder (ADD) and were prescribed stimulant medication. Attention Deficit Hyperactivity Disorder (ADHD) is characterized by problems in paying attention, excessive undirected activity, and poor school performance. After childhood trauma treatment, Ziegler reported that only about 5 percent still required stimulants.

Ziegler concluded, "Good trauma treatment often reduces or eliminates the symptoms and the need for medications. Always look for the cause behind the symptoms."

My two years working in the juvenile correctional institutional made a lasting imprint on my perspective of adult violence.

The boys were often engaging and genuinely charming. One beautiful, sunny crisp autumn day, I remember taking a break outside with some of the other staff. We stood next to the school building entrance and were laughing and joking around. The speech therapist, a plump, jolly blond woman in her mid-thirties, liked by both staff and students, called over three boys passing by on a sidewalk.

The speech therapist asked them to teach us, the staff, how to strut like a respected gang leader, a walk that when used in a violent neighborhood expressed toughness, a "nobody bother me" attitude, and general alpha male machismo.

Copying the strut took strict concentration. You had to stride with the left foot, and then as you moved your right foot, you needed to curve the right hand by the side, moving the wrist inward and down in a studied but seemingly relaxed style. One of the boys was a small but feisty twelve-year-old, muscular and compact, who patiently showed us how to walk while laughing at me and the other teachers when we tried to mimic him.

The memory is so vivid because the boys' faces were still so young and hopeful. They were just pretending to be hard and invulnerable. Later when I worked with vicious adult criminals, I was rarely afraid. In the eyes of the grown-up men, I'd see the shadow of their earlier selves. I'd see the child within.

In 1986, after six years as a public school psychologist, I returned to corrections to work again with Jo Ann Myrick, who was then running all EEN services within the adult prison system for seventeen- to twenty-one-year-old inmates. I was assigned to a medium-security prison at Kettle Moraine Correctional Institution (KMCI) in Plymouth, Wisconsin. I also traveled forty-five minutes once a week to Dodge Correctional Institution (DCI) in Waupun to screen new inmates under the age of twenty-one for special for special educational needs. I used my assessment skills learned in school psychology to assess the psychological needs of inmates entering the prison system for possible adjustment difficulties.

During my time at KMCI, I took extra graduate classes and passed the Examination for Professional Practices in Psychology (EPPP). I was awarded state certification for psychology. There was only a short period that the state granted these master's level psychology certificates, so I was very lucky.

Later, I took extra training in cognitive behavioral therapy and studied schema therapy with Jeff Young in 1994 when he came to speak in Madison and on a later occasion in Chicago. Young's theory seemed to explain the development of an abusive personality.

Young's theory of personality development describes the process by which violence is transmitted from one generation to the next. It explains why some children exposed to violence grow up to be violent offenders or abuse victims and why some children seem able to live a responsible, apparently normal adult life. The model identifies the basic transmission process by which a child chooses aggression as a legitimate way to solve life problems. The theory also explains why most adult survivors of childhood trauma, both violent and nonviolent, experience difficulties in intimate interpersonal relationships.

The model's key is the understanding that childhood trauma causes intense emotional pain and interferes with the child's normal and healthy emotional development. The child develops a distorted view of himself, others, and the world. "Am I good or bad? Are others good or bad?" This model is called *schema therapy* and is based on the belief that children make meaning of their experiences. The damage lies not so much in the specific experiences but how the child interpreted their relationships

Young's theory allows for different children based on their temperament to develop different patterns of behavior to the trauma. Some children externalize the emotional pain while others internalize into depression and self-hate. The child does what is necessary to survive. Some children will choose compliance to their abuser, another child fights back, a more aggressive child bullies other children, and yet another more passive child escapes mentally into video games or drugs.

The problem comes when the individual continues these distorted beliefs, irrational thinking, and problem behaviors into adulthood after they are no longer adaptive. Adult survivors develop a life trap—a lifelong pattern of thinking, feeling, and behaving that is self-defeating and destructive.

Violent offenders are different only by the way they reacted to the interpersonal trauma. They are not a different kind of animal or less human. The model presents the offender as an emotionally damaged individual. Not responsible for his own victimization; only responsible for changing his maladaptive behaviors.

The link between childhood abuse and neglect and the increased risk of later adult violence is documented in the *Adverse Childhood Experiences (ACES)* study from the 1990s, a collaboration between Kaiser Insurance and the Centers for Disease Control and Prevention (CDC). The study involved 77,000 adults who were middle class, middle aged, well-educated, and financially secure enough to have good medical insurance.

Between 1995 and 1997, the study researched the extent of trauma during childhood and correlated the intensity of the trauma with adult problem behaviors, known as *poor adult outcomes*, including depression, eating disorders, smoking, heart disease, cancer, stress, and alcoholism. Violence was only one subset of the numerous possible poor adult outcomes.

The ACES authors, Vincent Felitti and Robert Anda, developed ten questions carefully defining ten different categories of adverse childhood experiences. The research subjects responded to questions like "Did a parent or other adult in the household often or very often swear at you, insult or put you down?" and "As a child, did you witness your mother sometimes, often, or very often pushed, grabbed, slapped, or had something thrown at her?"

The categories of adverse childhood experiences included physical abuse and neglect, emotional abuse and neglect, and/or sexual abuse. The authors also included five factors assessing household dysfunction, including an absent parent, a mentally ill, addicted or incarcerated parent, and the witnessing of parental violence.

Respondents checked each type of traumatic circumstance occurring in his or her childhood. Each subject received an ACES score from one to ten, delineating the severity of childhood trauma. The ACES score was then analyzed and compared to the patient's medical and psychological history.

The ACES study found childhood traumatic experiences were much more common than originally expected, given that the sample of participants were mostly white, employed, and middle class. Twenty-eight percent of study participants reported physical abuse, and 21 percent reported sexual abuse.

Adverse childhood experiences often occurred together. Almost 40 percent of the original sample reported two or more ACES, and 12.5 percent experienced four or more. Because ACES occur in clusters, studies examined the cumulative effects of ACES rather than the individual effects of each.

The original ACES study found a dose-response relationship between childhood abuse and poor adult outcomes. A person's ACE score had a strong, graded relationship to poor adult outcomes including medical problems, such as diabetes, heart problems, and early death; social problems like poverty, homelessness, and unemployment; and mental health problems including depression, suicide attempts, and substance abuse.

The ACES study found four or more ACES in childhood increased by a factor of ten the risk of the individual becoming either a victim or perpetrator of domestic violence in adulthood.

The Adverse Childhood Experiences study (ACES) successfully documented the tremendous impact of childhood experiences on future violence victimization and perpetration and established childhood trauma as a public health issue. Yet initially, there was resistance to the idea of childhood origins of adult problems. The study began in an obesity clinic in San Diego. In 1985, Vincent Felitti developed a very successful weight loss program that helped people lose dramatic amounts of weight without surgery.

According to the story told by Bessel Van De Kolk in his book *The Body Keeps the Score,* Felitti was following up with a twenty-eight-year-old nurse's aide. She had gone from 408 pounds to 132 pounds. However, a few months later, she had regained an amazingly high amount of the weight back.

When Felitti inquired into what had happened, she told him that a male coworker had noticed her new figure and asked her out on a date. When the co-worker suggested sex, she went home and started eating and never stopped. Questioned further, she admitted to being sexually assaulted by her grandfather as a child.

After Felitti started questioning his other clients, he discovered that most of his morbidly obese clients shared similar experiences of sexual assault experiences as well as other family dysfunction. After he and his colleagues interviewed around 286 clients and found that most had been sexually abused as children, Felitti hypothesized that eating was a coping behavior for sexual abuse. Eating soothed anxiety and depression. Also, obese people were not seen as sexual objects, and by being fat, the clients felt more invisible and protected from harm.

In 1990, Felitti gave a speech in Atlanta proposing his new theory to a group of distinguished scientists and researchers studying the problem of obesity. Surprisingly, he was met with derision and criticism. The other experts thought the clients were lying about being abused in order to excuse their own failures to moderate their eating. Luckily, an epidemiologist from the CDC encouraged Felitti to start a much larger study, resulting in the extensive ACES study.

When I returned to corrections, this time in the adult system in 1986, there was a pervasive philosophy that offenders should not discuss their childhoods, no matter how traumatic. Just like the obese patients in Felitti's first study, childhood trauma was seen as an excuse for poor behavior. Inmates were told that since not everyone who suffered childhood abuse became a criminal, it was the inmate's choice and failing.

This approach seemed shame-based to me. Offenders were told, "You are bad and you need to admit it." I thought it would be better to help the offender understand the link between their childhood experiences and their adult problem behavior, including other destructive patterns like drug addiction, gambling, and shoplifting. As a primary example, we see that Oprah as a survivor of sexual abuse overeats; the domestically violent abuser uses violence.

Explaining and understanding are not excusing or justifying. The offenders were unable to learn from their negative consequences. They continued to repeat the same behaviors expecting different results. Instead of blaming or shaming, the concept of life traps allows the individual to objectively analyze what went wrong and try to fix it.

My interest in Jeff Young's idea of a life trap was personal as well as professional. As I attended graduate school and started working as a school psychologist, I was stuck in my own life trap. I was an attractive, bright, and interesting woman. Yet I continued a repetitive and self-defeating cycle of unhealthy relationships that I could not break out of.

As soon as I entered a relationship with an eligible man, I would immediately come to believe that I had met my soul mate, that we would eventually marry and live happily ever after. I was very anxious that he would reject or leave me and, consequently, I would never be happy again. My behavior would become clingy and smothering. I would lose my friends and interests, taking on his life and changing myself to be someone I thought he could love.

The relationship would end with my boyfriend dumping me. I would have difficulty letting go of the relationship and would become depressed. Finally, I would pull myself out of my depression and then begin to attract men again. The pattern was repeated. I knew my behavior was pushing my intimate partners away, but I couldn't stop. I was too irrational. I was too afraid to be alone.

Analyzing my own dysfunctional relationship patterns using Jeff Young's schema therapy, found in his self-help book *Reinventing Your Life: How to Break Free from Negative Life Patterns and Feel Good Again,* I also found compassion for the offenders who prevented themselves from a life of intimacy and love by using aggression.

Compassion as defined by psychologist Steven Stosny in *Treating Attachment Abuse: A Compassionate Approach* implies equality: "I sympathize with your hurt because despite differences in luck, we are (humanely) equal." Compassion for others empowers the self through the experience of understanding, sympathy, and support.

While working part-time at Taycheedah Correctional Institution, a Wisconsin's women's prison located in Fond du lac, Wisconsin, as a school psychologist in 1986, I met a female inmate named Jane, a woman my own age, of similar build and appearance. She was incarcerated for helping her boyfriend rob a pharmacy for drugs. She fell into an abusive relationship with a similar pattern to my own unhealthy relationships. She would do anything to keep him from leaving her and changed her identity to meet what he wanted.

Of course, my life trap was less severe and less damaging than Jane's, but I was reminded of a sixteenth-century proverb by John Bradford as he watched a group of prisoners being led to execution: "There but for the grace of fortune, go I."

CHAPTER 1

Michael and C-PTSD

Michael hated everyone. He was a forty-seven-year-old three-time felon in prison for assault offenses: two battery charges on two different wives and then taking a hatchet to a stranger in the street. He never sought help from psychological services. Michael believed therapy was a waste of time. He thought anyone who sought therapy was "weak" and he did not trust anyone anyway.

Michael saw himself as independent, self-reliant, needing no one. Michael spent his free time pacing in his small cell. He stopped going to the library and chapel services. While he had been never been violent in the prison setting, he was irritable and defensive. Verbal confrontations with staff and other inmates became a common occurrence. Frequently at night, Michael awoke screaming, shaking, and trembling in his flimsy bunk bed, haunted by violent nightmares. His cellmate finally told him, "Dude, you need help."

The year was 2010. I had been at Fox Lake Correctional Institution (FLCI) for fifteen years as a clinical psychologist. Fox Lake was a small medium-security prison run by the Wisconsin Department of Corrections. It was constructed in the middle of cornfields, outside the Town of Fox Lake, population 1,519. The compound was fifteen flat acres of cottages and administration buildings, enclosed by two razor-wired and electrified fences.

The inmate population then was 1,100. Psychological services at FLCI had only three clinicians. Part of our being understaffed was due to severely mentally ill and aggressive inmates being sent to FLCI because of overcrowding elsewhere in the state. Further, for the first time in seven years, I was getting a supervisor. The prison's human resources staff and the warden had finally found a PhD to fill the vacant position.

I was used to performing my duties without much direction. The other medium-security prisons, like Oshkosh CI or Kettle Moraine CI, each had a supervisor who met a few times a year at the department's central office in Madison to discuss important issues and new policies. Each month seemed to bring new restrictions, more paperwork, and added expectations from central office. I was used to doing my own thing. And now I was going to have a supervisor who would make sure I followed every last policy and procedure, regardless if it worked against my relationships with inmates.

Michael finally wrote a request for an interview with psychological services, and I was assigned to his case. I called him up to my office in the administration building to interview him, assess his clinical issues, set up a treatment plan, and write a report with recommendations.

The atmosphere at FLCI was much more relaxed than a typical penal institution. Inmates were allowed to walk unescorted from their cottage housing to school or chapel on sidewalks surrounded by carefully manicured lawns. There were areas outside of the units with basketball hoops and picnic benches where the inmates could relax in nice weather.

My office was as inviting as I could make it under the conditions. The building was built in 1968, had paper-thin walls, and the antiquated heating made some of the offices feel like saunas and others like walk-in freezers. Luckily, for the summer heat, I did have my own air conditioner, which was maintained by the inmate students in the HVAC Vocational program. Posters, pictures, and a dried flower wreath decorated the walls. A handmade quilt was thrown over the extra client chair.

FLCI was called a "responsible living" prison. Residents had demonstrated an ability to adjust with fewer restrictions than a maximum-security prison. However, policies and procedures still controlled the inmates' movements. Inmates signed in and out of their school or work assignments and were identified by security staff as usually conforming or potentially violent.

There were two inmates in each 12 by 8 foot cell. Each inmate slept on a bunk bed embedded into the concrete wall and had use of half of a desk and a locked box. The prison added two barracks due to overcrowding, where prisoners had even less privacy.

There were rules for foot traffic, for eating in the unit chow hall and almost every other situation. If there was an infraction, the inmate received a conduct report. If minor, the punishment was a loss of recreation or room confinement; if major, the inmate might be placed in the segregation building with even more rules.

Michael entered my office for the first time, not happy about having to talk to a shrink. His hostility crackled like electricity, and he stared at me with an angry look. His left leg jittered up and down, and his eyes darted around the office searching for signs of threat. His reluctance to talk to me was very clear. Michael jerked at every sound and was distracted by others walking in the hallway outside my door.

An initial diagnosis seemed fairly clear: Post-Traumatic Stress Disorder (PTSD). Michael showed the hypervigilance, anxiety, and physiological arousal common to victims of trauma. He also complained of difficulties sleeping, panic attacks when in crowded spaces, and his mood was always irritable.

Speaking in a low, monotone voice, his affect flat but insistent, Michael decided, after some minutes of getting to know me, to tell me a story.

During his junior year in high school, Michael was walking with a friend on a New York City street to the local McDonald's when a car pulled up. Shots were fired, and his friend collapsed, a bullet in the head. After the horrific event, Michael reported violent nightmares and flashback images of his friend's brain splattered across the sidewalk.

A knot in his stomach relayed the message of danger, as his brain informed his body to get ready for "fight/flight." Heart rate increases, breathing becomes shallow, blood is transferred from the brain to the large muscles to prepare the individual to respond quickly.

After a trauma, the human body continues in this survival mode long after the danger has passed. The brain becomes trained to not miss any signs of potential danger, so the high arousal state dominates. The individual's mood is colored by this negative energy.

Each week at FLCI, the clinical psychologists met with a state-hired psychiatrist who came to the institution to prescribe medications and monitor inmates. Fortunately, our assigned psychiatrist was smart, funny, and interested in our non-psychiatric opinion of the inmates and our recommendations for treatment.

I presented Michael's case in a conference, noting his PTSD symptoms after the street violence he experienced. I asked the psychiatrist whether medication should be discussed to lower Michael's arousal level and to help him get to sleep at night. This way, during the day, he would feel less like jumping out of his skin. Our psychiatrist had mentioned previously a new drug helping combat veterans with nightmares.

I asked if Michael should have a psychiatric referral.

"But don't forget that Michael is an antisocial personality," Dr. Black, my new supervisor, said.

Dr. Black was an overweight older psychologist who had recently transferred from a high security institution. He tended to see the inmates as more criminal than mentally ill. He thought most clients were malingering to get social security benefits.

Antisocial personality disorder (ASPD) was an important diagnosis for Michael. A personality disorder is defined as a mental health condition that exhibits a long-term pattern of behaviors, emotions, and thoughts that are different from the culture's expectations. These behaviors interfere with the person's ability to function in relationships, work, and other settings.

Antisocial personality disorder is a pervasive pattern of disregard for or violations of the rights of others. Symptoms of ASPD are mostly behavioral, including a history of crime, legal problems, and failure to be responsible in society or impulsive and aggressive behavior.

I agreed with Dr. Black that Michael's history met the criteria for ASPD. But I argued with his assumption that antisocial personalities were necessarily trying to lie and manipulate others. Unfortunately, there was an even more pervasive suggestion that the antisocial personality diagnosis meant the person was evil, someone who chose to hurt others in a rational process to serve his or her own self-interest. I know there are offenders with these qualities. I just did not believe Michael was one of them.

I knew Michael was not a pleasant person. When anyone, inmate or staff, annoyed him in any way, he informed me, "I want to take a bat and beat him." He had no friends. He was prickly with other inmates. His defensiveness was like quills on a porcupine, ready to aggressively protect itself at any moment.

Even the most understanding staff person had a limit to the patience that could be shown to inmates. I admit that I often became annoyed with Michael due to his constant complaining. If I didn't redirect him, he spent our therapy sessions accusing security officers of malicious intent or disparaging his fellow inmates. He summarized his inability to get along with others in a simple slogan: "I don't do stupid."

As a result, when Michael described a conflict he experienced in the unit or at school, everyone else was always to blame. He regularly expected others to manipulate, humiliate, or betray him. At times, I reminded Michael of others he had known, like a previous female teacher who had, by his own words, shown him some kindness.

Michael rejected his own memory by pessimistically saying, "She just hasn't had the chance to hurt me."

There was no argument that Michael's scornful behavior made him an outcast at the institution. No one tried to suggest he was a likeable personality. But I just chafed at the assumption that he was to be written off as a person with little value to humanity, not worth my clinical attention.

The tension between Dr. Black and me increased. He questioned the veracity of everything Michael had told me. The traumatic shooting was not documented in Michael's social service file.

Dr. Black asked me, "How do we know this even happened?"

I insisted that everything about Michael's behavior suggested he was affected by the shooting.

"Offenders lie," Dr. Black glibly replied. "Michael was probably in a gang. He was part of the violence. He's not the victim."

Even worse, when I requested that Michael be given medication to deal with his anxiety, I was summarily dismissed.

"Anti-anxiety medications are highly addictive," Dr. Black blithely announced. "Michael is malingering. He's feigning anxiety symptoms in order to obtain drugs he can use to get high or sell on the prison black market. He's manipulating you, Linda. Michael will use you for sympathy and attention."

I believed my supervisor to be wrong. In Michael's case, he was not willing to budge. His mind was set. To Dr. Black, Michael was an antisocial, probably psychopathic deviant who wanted to manipulate me for his own benefit. There was some research that suggested an antisocial personality can get worse with treatment, making Michael a poor treatment candidate. Dr. Black wanted me to limit my time with Michael.

I had another explanation for Michael's antisocial attitudes, beliefs, and behaviors. As a victim of childhood trauma, he developed an antisocial personality to survive in the toxic environment. Michael's horrible childhood was not an excuse, but it provided an explanation. Michael's attitude and behavior made even more sense when I spent additional time with him and learned more about his history.

When Michael was aged five, I found out, his mother had tried to kill him. She gave him some pills, took pills herself, and lay next to him on the bed. The paramedics broke down the locked bedroom door and were able to save the child's life. His mother was already dead.

Michael did not remember much about his life before that terrifying moment. When I asked him how he felt, knowing that his mother tried to kill him, Michael clearly indicated he believed his life was not worth saving.

"I should have died with my mother," he told me.

He confided that an older sister took custody. But this did not improve his life. Michael and his sister's three children were taken out of the new home on several occasions due to his sister's neglect and abuse. He experienced the additional trauma of watching his sister beaten by her boyfriends with the police called. It is likely that the sister's boyfriend saw Michael as an obstacle, a rival for the sister's attention, rather than a sibling needing guidance and protection.

Michael, when I prodded him, did not remember any positive and loving interactions in his past family dynamics. He had only a faint memory of being hugged by a grandmother before his mother tried to kill him and died.

"I tried to run away a few times," Michael recalled of the time when he lived with his sister. "But I was always returned to her house.

"She just wanted the money from the state," he stated flatly. "She didn't want me."

Michael's mind was so filled with revulsion for his past that even when I encouraged and helped him, negativity still controlled his thoughts. Once, while we worked on a plan for his release, Michael's features suddenly turned dark and foreboding.

"I know I'll fail just like everyone told me."

"Who told you that?" I asked.

"Everyone." I saw his face registering memories. Perhaps he was flashing back to being criticized by teachers. Perhaps he saw the face of disgust on the policeman's face when Michael was caught running away. Perhaps he remembered his sister or her boyfriend's telling him he would not amount to anything.

Adverse memories accumulate, and the child makes unconscious conclusions. Michael's beliefs were distorted by his experience of people consistently hurting him. No one showed unconditional love to him, so tragically, it made sense for Michael to be defensive, angry, and ready to hurt others, assuming they were going to hurt him first.

To most people, memory is defined as consciously recalling an event from the past. We usually think of memory as facts. What did you eat last Sunday? Who was the first American president? What are the names of the planets in our solar system? What was the instruction your coworker gave you last week? What was on that grocery list?

This kind of memory is explicit. It's intentional and conscious. The memories can be dissected and revisualized and perhaps even laughed at with emotional distance as you experience again your memory of swimming last summer. But the person who was with you may have a different version of the event. Your memory is really a sense of remembering, an awareness of the event that occurred in the past. It is not a video or photographic recreation of that event.

Explicit memories form in the child's cortex, a part of the brain dedicated to learning, reasoning, and logic. Explicit memories do not begin to develop in a child until he learns language, from ages one to three. Difficulty recalling the first few years of life is called childhood amnesia.

Implicit memory is stored in the amygdala, the part of the brain that is centered on survival. This brain area is wired to leap into action at birth. Implicit memory presents itself in the form of simple associations, such as a toddler frightened by a loud noise associated with a toy. As a result of the implicit memory, the toddler will get upset when he or she sees the toy in the future. No conscious, verbal, or logical reasoning is connected to this reaction. The cerebral networks automatically link the visual stimulus to the emotional reaction.

Traumatic memories are implicit. A memory of a car accident consists of fragmented moments, like seeing the other car coming toward you, the sound of the screech of the brakes or the crash, and bodily sensations like being thrown against the car window.

Experiences of terror, fear, humiliation, or shame can be recalled as an implicit memory without the individual's explicit memory of the same event. In essence, it can be an emotional flashback, with no sense of a visual event being recalled. The emotional state is experienced as a current reality. If this emotion lasts over time, it becomes a mood.

Repeated experiences become ingrained in the circuits of the brain as states of mind. The mood shapes the way the individual processes information from the environment.

As a child, Michael experienced many times being rejected, so that eventually it became a mood, an emotion that felt real to him. It didn't feel like a memory. The emotional pain was his reality. He fought against the negative emotion of rejection with anger. His emotional response from past experiences was, as a default position, anger. In essence, his motto could be described as, "You're not going to reject me, because I'll reject you first."

Michael, even as an adult, still perceived other people's behavior as constant signs of rejection. His mood slanted his evaluations of potential friends and ignited the belief that others couldn't be trusted.

Michael's antisocial attitudes, beliefs, and moods were a response to his early trauma. Even though I could not convince Dr. Black at FLCI of it, his true diagnosis should have been Complex-Post Traumatic Stress Disorder (C-PTSD).

The symptoms of C-PTSD include the physical symptoms of simple PTSD, that is, the reexperiencing of trauma, leading to hyperarousal and irritability.

Complex PTSD as a diagnosis also includes the impact the trauma had on the child's normal developmental process. A child raised in a toxic family should be seen as damaged neurologically, emotionally, and socially.

My weekly meetings with Michael became more important to him. They also elevated my own need to feel like I was helping others, not just being a cog in a machine. I noted that he became eager to see me, and he seemed a little more relaxed and less quick to get defensive. Michael, instead of merely cooperating and telling me of his history when I asked, began to desire to tell stories about his past experiences of being abused. When I expressed anger at how he was victimized as a child, both verbally and physically, he clearly appreciated it, and it spurred him to open up to me more.

But despite this developing bond of trust, Michael avoided talking about his sister in detail, even though he admitted she was the person "who I called my mother." He didn't know where she was. She had never contacted him since he was sentenced to prison. I got the impression, although I could not be sure, that Michael as an adult had been physically aggressive, at least one time, with his sister-mother. But even with his more relaxed demeanor, Michael adamantly refused to talk about her with any depth, and I knew, at that point, it would set back our progress if I pushed him.

It was nearing Christmas. I had been working with Michael for about five months. Because holidays in prison were difficult, even for the most hardened offender, another inmate in the unit told Michael that he had used the Internet to locate Michael's sister. The friend's family had put a notice on the Web asking anyone to respond if they were related to Michael. As a result, a woman in Milwaukee, claiming to be Michael's sister, posted her own location information.

Michael, at first, expressed excitement. At our next session, he admitted to writing a Christmas card to her. He seemed angry at himself for desiring her response. He expected her to reject him and mad at himself for opening himself up to be hurt.

And sure enough, his fear became reality. A response never came. Each week, Michael painfully admitted that she had not yet written back. Michael seemed hopeless. The first response to rejection is usually a feeling of personal inadequacy. Michael avoided the feelings of vulnerability with anger. He blamed her for being thoughtless and cruel.

I tried, in the sessions that followed, to find an alternative explanation for her lack of response. I said that I couldn't figure out why she would write her address on the Internet and then not follow through on his letter to her. This kind of behavior was so different from my own family experience.

"She might have given up on you because you keep returning to prison," I suggested. Many families get tired of the offender's excuses and justifications and finally make him an outcast. I worked with Michael to distinguish between rejections due to one's behavior versus a rejection of a person's intrinsic worth.

I also jumped at the chance to provide in as gentle a manner as possible the evidence for the following truism: if you abuse people, then they will not want to be around you. Everything I had learned thus far about Michael suggested he was unaware of the cause and effect concept in human relationships. He did not see himself as others did. I hoped that he would volunteer information about any violence between him and his sister who had acted as his mother.

And then, Michael threw me a curve. Instead of talking more about his sister, he revealed information about a brother who had gone undiscussed up to that point. After being witness to his friend's street shooting, Michael, then a junior in high school, was thrown out of his sister's violent home environment to stay with his brother, who lived in the Midwest.

As Michael told me the story, I found myself surprised. It appeared that the family had attempted to intervene in Michael's downward track toward crime by having him move in with a brother who was stable and responsible. Michael's brother had escaped their dysfunctional family by joining the military. His brother set firm rules for Michael if he was to remain in the home.

At first, Michael did really well. He responded positively to the structured environment and found that he enjoyed positive attention. He remembered getting a trophy for some martial arts class he had taken and getting an acknowledgment from his brother.

"I felt great when he smiled at me and seemed so proud," Michael recalled, and he puffed out his chest ever so slightly as he shared this memory with me. It was a rare happy moment, along with the vague memory of his grandmother hugging him that Michael savored.

I asked him why he didn't stay with his brother longer than the nine months he had mentioned. Michael described testing his brother's rules and limits. He started hanging out with his friends after the curfew his brother had imposed.

He described the incident triggering his return to his sister's home in a way that made it seem incidental, unimportant. "I went out without my brother's permission. My brother and his wife had gone out for the evening. I took his car without permission and got into a fender bender."

I questioned Michael's perception of the crash as a "fender bender." Michael had a built-in bias. Possibly, the car accident was major, seriously damaging the car, raising his brother's insurance and putting him in legal jeopardy. On the other hand, Michael's brother may have been overly rigid with his rules and could have given Michael a second chance.

Whatever the truth of the matter was, the result was sadly familiar. Asked to leave his brother's house, Michael returned to the city, quit school, and started living in the streets. Michael's self-defeating behavioral pattern was well set by that time. This experience reinforced an already well-established belief that the world was out to get him.

Michael was bitter about the experience and blamed his brother. "He didn't give me a chance," Michael said of his brother. His brother's rejection of him reinforced Michael's belief that he never got a break and no one cared.

Michael implicitly believed, in his emotional reality, that his sister and his older brother both hated him. He was convinced of these beliefs. They were a core part of Michael's identity.

I wanted to provide an alternative explanation for his sister's lack of response to his letter. But after discussing his past stay with his brother and coming to understand his sister was not going to write to him, Michael's behavior in our sessions took a dramatic and frightening turn for the worse.

One day, as he reflected on his sister's failure to write to him, he exploded. Michael continued to sit in his chair in front of my desk, but his movements became frantic and disorganized. His focus shifted, he acted like I was no longer there, and he was talking directly to his sister in the room.

Adding to this disturbing scenario was the vulgar, violent language he used. Michael's fury was so great that he was conjuring up things he wanted to see done to his sister, images that the worst horror movie would think twice about using. I was stunned.

Michael mixed up his present and past tenses as he raged. It sounded like he was describing a past violent episode with his sister and then fantasizing a future one. I could not verbally get him to stop.

I was awestruck at the depth of Michael's anguish, the intensity of his anger. I believed Michael when he said he wanted to kill his sister. I felt sure that he had been violent to her in the past.

I don't think he was even aware then of being in my office. He was experiencing an implicit memory, a flashback to a previous rejection. It was an emotional flashback. He was ready to fight.

It was difficult to calm him down. Finally, he realized that he was in my office, in no threat, and I sent him back to his cell. After he was gone, I began to wonder, How responsible was Michael for his very intense, out-of-control aggressive responses? I tended to hold offenders responsible whenever they chose violence. But I reevaluated my opinion, watching Michael's behavior that day.

Daniel Siegel, a neurobiologist, in his book *The Developing Mind,* describes the brain experiencing a physiological arousal level so intense that a flood of energy may bombard the mind and take over a number of processes, ranging from rational thinking to social behavior. At this point, emotions may overtake conscious awareness.

"Some have called this an emotional 'hijacking,' 'breakdown,' or 'flooding.' In such a situation, one's behavior may no longer feel volitional and thoughts may feel out of control.

"Images may fill the mind's eye with visual representations symbolic of emotional sensation. For example, when angry, some people may 'see red' or visualize doing harm to the target of their rage. They may lose control of their behavior, performing destructive acts that would not be part of their behavioral repertoires under 'normal conditions.'"

My supervisor characterized Michael simply as just an antisocial personality, all about personal gain and manipulation. More than ever, I disagreed and saw Michael with complex PTSD. I didn't think Michael was completely responsible for his behavior. It would not be the only time that in my position as psychologist I felt we failed to help an inmate who required special care.

CHAPTER 2

Derek and His Life Traps

I met Derek when he was suicidal. Derek was a thirty-seven-year old black inmate was incarcerated for violently assaulting Tamika, his girlfriend of eight years. Derek explained his self-hatred at our first interaction, in my office: "I remember watching my stepfather beat my mother. I would sit in my room with my hands over my ears. I promised myself I would never act like that. Now I'm the monster."

I worked with Derek for two years. For the first ten months, I saw Derek in individual therapy. During the second year, Derek was a participant in my year-long, offense-related treatment group. The treatment was structured and included an educational component aimed at teaching the science of personality. I applied Jeff Young's schema therapy, which gained acceptance after the publication of *Schema Therapy; A Practitioner's Guide*. It gave guidelines on how the offender can focus directly on stopping interpersonal violence.

Derek was a hefty inmate, broad-shouldered but with muscles no longer toned, like an out-of-shape football player. He was large but gentle, walking with his head slightly bowed and a lumbering gait.

In my office, Derek's affect was sad and flat; his mood was depressed. He spoke in a soft monotone voice. He gave the impression that talking to me took a lot of energy and was an extreme effort.

Derek was highly self-critical, right from the first session. "I'm worth nothing," he intoned, defeated. "I deserve punishment. I am scum."

"But you can change," I urged him. "You can become a better person." I believed therapy to be a redemptive process. In the Hebrew language, the word for repentance is *teshuva*, a remaking of the self. I explained to him that in the therapy process, you review your life mistakes, understand the life experiences that taught you to be self-defeating and hurtful, and then, you identify the values and beliefs that will help you be the person you want to be.

Derek was not easily convinced that he could have a better life. He recalled his relationship with Tamika. He said to me, "I tried to change. Things went well for a while. Then I started to treat her like shit because I didn't feel good about myself. I started by degrading her, by calling her names and yelling at her. Eventually, the worse I felt about myself, the worse I treated her. I see that now, but at the time, it was all her fault. It started out with verbal abuse and emotional then turned into physical. After the physical situations, I truly felt bad about it but if something wasn't right, I'd slip back into my old ways."

Derek described what we call a life trap. His habits of illogical thinking, emotional overreactions, and irrational behavior were developed in response to an abusive and neglectful family upbringing. Derek continued this pattern into adulthood. It may have helped him cope with his childhood, but clearly, it wound up actively disrupting his ability to function in society.

The concept of a life trap, a lifelong vicious cycle of trying to change and make a better life but only repeating the misery of childhood, is not exactly new.

Sigmund Freud, the Father of Psychoanalysis, observed that his clients found themselves in self-defeating life patterns, "repeating the pain of our childhood." Freud's psychological term was repetition-compulsion and was explained by the individual's unconscious mind influencing his or her behavior without the individual's awareness or intention.

The term *life trap* was popularized in Jeff Young and Janet Klosko's book, *Reinventing Your Life: The Breakthrough Program End Negative Behavior and Feel Great Again.* The term *life trap* imaginatively suggests the image of a quagmire, a giant pit, one you pull yourself out of but then get pulled back down.

Examples of real-world life traps are setting yourself up for failure by getting drawn into unhealthy relationships, such as those with emotionally unstable or unavailable partners or finding oneself fired for the thirteenth time.

The idea of a life trap, repeating the same behavior but expecting different results, was all too familiar to me in my own life. I had already observed my own self-defeating patterns in romantic relationships. Outwardly, I presented myself as a free spirit who was independent and did not need to be married. But the actual results told a different story. I jumped into intimacy, became needy and suffocating, set the relationship up to fail, and then had difficulty letting go.

My own life trap's theme is, I recognized, fear of abandonment. It probably originated in an unintended separation from my parents at age three. I was hospitalized for observation due to what turned out to be an innocent heart murmur. At the time, I didn't feel sick and my child mind could not figure out why I couldn't go home to my family. When a freak spring snowstorm paralyzed my small Pennsylvania town, my parents were unable to come and visit me.

In Young's book, The *Schema Therapy Clinicians Guide*, the schema is a scientific term to mean "a broad, organizing principle, a mental model, outline or framework for making sense of one's experience." A maladaptive schema is developed from repeated adverse childhood experiences. The schema develops from repeated traumatic experiences and is stored in the amygdala, the brain's center of emotions, as an implicit memory. Through this process, the individual interprets reality through a distorted lens.

So in my own case, as a three-year-old child, the schema became a fear. Abandonment in a hospital without the presence of my parents became the belief "I am alone and I'll die." The schema becomes part of one's identity and triggers a spike in anxiety and increases the risk of acting impulsively.

The core belief of the abandonment schema can be stated this way: "In the end, either by your dying, sending me away or leaving, I will be alone."

If the negative schema survives, it does so because it is reinforced and elaborated on by later life experiences that seem to fit it. For example, as I engaged in a series of short-term romances, my mind highlighted memories of men who had dumped me. At the same time, I avoided thinking deeply about situations when I had rejected a possible mate for not being appropriate for me. Even if I didn't really care a great deal about losing a particular partner in a broken relationship, I overreacted as if it was the end of my world. Each breakup provided, to my mind, additional evidence that I would never find a soul mate and would die an old maid.

The schema model explained my self-defeating life patterns: Negative experience leads to distorted beliefs, these beliefs trigger a lot of anxiety, and anxiety leads to impulsive behavior and overly emotional decision-making, which results in one recreating the negative dramas of the past. The pattern repeats.

Because life traps find their origins in childhood experiences, I believed that reviewing an offender's childhood was necessary for emotional healing and growth. Explicit memories of what really happened were not important; the child's implicit learning from major negative events formed his maladaptive schema.

To me, a schema therapy model gave me a diagram to analyze and decode my own behavior. I thought helping Derek figure out his life traps might help illuminate how he kept failing in relationships. But he had to be willing to face them, acknowledge their existence first.

In the life trap curriculum I created for the Department of Corrections, I asked each treatment participant to share an explicit memory from his childhood. When Derek's turn came and the group turned to him, his facial expression became one of embarrassment. It was as if he wanted to say aloud, "No one would want to hear what I have to say."

Derek had been in the same group of ten inmates, along with a co-facilitator and social worker, Don, and me for six months. By that time, despite his affected chagrin, Derek knew his responses would be encouraged and supported. And Derek was well-liked by the others in the group. He had a shy smile, a warm laugh, and was a pleasant change from the many angry inmates I worked with over time.

The task of the group was well-defined. They were asked to listen to an objective memory from Derek, told as a narrative. Then they would be allowed to ask Derek questions to get more details about the experience. Finally, anyone could offer to help Derek identify the possible life traps that were either started or reinforced by the traumatic incident.

Derek looked around the room at us all and then began. "One morning, my stepfather called to my sister, 'Come do the dishes.' She started crying because we knew what that meant. She was about to be sexually abused. I said to him, 'Leave my sister alone.' He smacked me so hard blood came to my mouth. But I didn't let my sister go. My two brothers woke up to help. So he finally left the house. We had won that morning."

"Later that day, he came back with an electric extension cord in his hand and started slashing me with it. I tried to run but he blocked my way and forced me into a corner. He got a crazy look on his face and started beating me over and over. I wished I had gun to shoot him. He said 'Boy, I'm going to teach you a lesson you'll never forget.'"

"What were the feelings?" I asked very cautiously.

"I felt paralyzed, weak. He was in control. He kept hitting me until I finally forgot any pride I ever had and begged him to stop." Derek grew agitated. Some of the other group members nodded with recognition.

"My dad said the same thing," one of the other men admitted, "about teaching me a lesson." This offender had also been physically abused by his father. Of the ten inmates in the treatment group, each one had a documented history of physical abuse against him, usually by an authority figure.

I tried to visualize how these men might have felt as children—being beaten, kicked, hit with a belt, facing the possibility of serious injury or even death. But since I have never been physically attacked or threatened in my life, my imagination failed.

None of Jeff Young's eighteen identified early maladaptive schemas (EMS) or life traps seemed to capture the essence of the emotional pain caused by being forced to submit to the will of another person. The experience takes away all sense of agency and control, leaving the victim disempowered and helpless.

I decided to call this life trap *powerlessness.* The schema is a distorted belief developed in a toxic situation. As a child, Derek did not have any power. His stepfather controlled him. Derek's belief system could be summed up as "I am without control."

Derek's way of coping with feeling defenseless and vulnerability was to *counterattack,* to fight the schema by convincing himself and everyone else around him that the opposite of the schema was true, that not only was he not weak and submissive, but also, despite appearances, he was the one in control.

"Even when my stepfather was beating me into a pulp," he told us all, an edge coming into his otherwise steady voice, "in my head, I felt in control. I wanted to kill that motherfucker. I'd imagine me getting revenge. I had fantasies of my getting a gun and shooting him or just using my fists so I could feel my fist hitting his face."

Derek continued, seeing the link from his experiences as a victim of physical violence to his aggressive behavior.

"At home, we never knew when my stepfather was going to come home and beat someone. So I went to school and became a bully. As I got older, I would go to a bar and pick a fight just so I could show I was stronger and more powerful.

"With Tamika, I controlled everything she did. She couldn't go anywhere without asking me first. I'd call her all kinds of names and told her she was fat and that I was going to sleep with one of her friends. I'd threaten her with violence if she didn't do things my way."

It felt like no one was breathing in the room. In addition to his harsh story of being abused, Derek decided to turn his attention to another type of trauma in his childhood. As a child, Derek was also forced to listen to or watch his stepfather violently attack his mother.

Derek said, "Watching my mother being beat was worse than being hit myself. I couldn't protect her. I was a coward. I blamed myself for her getting hurt."

I listened to Derek's words and understood why he felt that way, and yet, at the same time, I knew it was wrong, that he was unfairly punishing himself. Derek was only an innocent observer. How did Derek's anger at his stepfather transfer to anger at himself?

Derek's self-blame and poor reasoning was typical of men who are abused as children and became violent as adults. Sociologist Lonnie Athens, in his book *The Creation of Dangerous, Violent Criminals*, interviewed prisoners convicted of the most heinous crimes. Athens described common psychological responses to a brutalizing family environment.

Athens summarized twenty years of his interviews with incarcerated murderers and rapists, examining the similar childhood experiences these violent men shared. The term Athens created for the trauma of witnessing parental violence was *personal horrification*.

In such a terrifying scene as the one Derek experienced, the child watches his mother being thrown around the room by his stepfather and the action seems to be in slow motion. The child fears for the safety of the mother. He feels a powerful urge to intervene and physically attack his mother's aggressor.

The child calculates the chances of successfully confronting the aggressor as low and the possible negative consequences to himself as severe. His fear for his own safety overrides his desire to protect her. Not surprisingly, the child fails to act.

Athens wrote, "The child is overcome with feelings of impotence ... and mistakenly concludes that it is his own impotence rather than the aggressor's wickedness which was primarily responsible for the episode of violence .... No matter how right or wrong his reasoning is, the end result is the same; he feels intense shame."

The experience of personal horrification causes the child to develop a defectiveness/shame life trap. The core belief of this schema is "I am inadequate. I have no value, no worth. I'm broken. No one will ever love me."

Victims of trauma often blame themselves for the abuse they witness, leading to a schema of defectiveness/shame. At the time Derek was abusing Tamika, he showed no outward sign of this self-hatred. He presented as confident, arrogant, and narcissistic. But inside, he felt self-loathing.

"I felt like a shit," Derek confirmed to us, still rapt, unable to move. "I felt the worst with Tamika because just looking at her reminded me what a shit I was." Tamika was like a broken mirror to Derek. Instead of reflecting a positive sense of self, all he could see in her eyes was shame.

There was a break in his painful admission. I asked Derek, "How did you cope?"

"I tried to escape the pain. I told Tamika I was going to work. But I never went. I'd go to the band and get money and buy drugs and alcohol and pick up a woman to go to the hotel all day long. Sex, drugs, and violence. I didn't care about anything except making myself feel good, even for a moment."

Derek reflected on his life trap. "Because of my past trauma, I didn't see the world right. I focused on control and felt so bad about myself I would either try to make Tamika feel bad, put her down so I'd feel better, or I'd run away and try to escape."

After that emotional yet highly productive session, Derek seemed more content as we worked together in the group to understand how his childhood influenced his adult world. The shame he carried around with him all the time seemed diminished.

At the next group that involved Derek, I presented the treatment as problem-solving. I told Derek he had a life problem and the process of talking about his past was the way he developed the skill of finding solutions.

His confidence and willingness to talk had increased since the time. "The worst memory," he began bravely that day, "involves my mother going away, leaving me alone. I remember sitting at the top of the stairs when I around five years old, staring at the door waiting for her to come home.

"I know now she was forced to run away for her own safety. But all I remember is the feeling of abandonment. I was afraid she would never come back and wondering how she could leave me if she loved me."

Derek did not remember how often she left or how long she was gone during that specific incident. "It seemed like forever," he said to the group. The schema had no sense of past, present, or future.

"How did abandonment color your relationship with Tamika?" I wanted him to relate that childhood memory to his own violence.

"I was always afraid Tamika would leave me. I controlled where she went, whom she'd see, making sure she didn't have a chance to meet other men who might take her away. I was insanely jealous."

Jealousy seemed to be a universally acknowledged issue in domestically violent relationships. I told the group that in one of my previous groups, an inmate admitted he would sniff his girlfriend's panties at night to see if she had had sex with someone else during the day.

"I wasn't that bad," Derek assured everyone, garnering a few chuckles from the other offenders. "But I did monitor her mail and would sneak inside her cell phone records to see whom she'd called. I'd imagine she was sleeping around, even convinced myself that she must be cheating. I'd accuse her. If she denied it, I'd call her a liar."

Although conjugal jealousy was a familiar pattern in the domestically violent offender, there could be different schemas operating. I used a technique called vertical arrow questioning to uncover the organizing theme.

"Suppose she *was* cheating," I suggested. "Why would that be so bad?" This form of questioning ran the risk of angering the offender. But it had the potential for great self-revelation too. Of course, a simple answer, in fact, an avoidance of an answer, would be to say, "No one wants a partner to cheat." But my intent was to get to the acknowledgment that not everyone decides violence is necessary to prevent infidelity. What was so important to Derek? What would her cheating mean about him?

Derek did not raise his voice or grow tense. He looked me right in the eye after I asked him what Tamika's theoretical cheating would mean and said, "I'm not good enough for her and she'll hook up with that other guy."

I appreciated his honesty, but there was a deeper truth he was not speaking aloud. "Why would that be so bad?" I asked. "What would that mean about you?"

"I'll be alone." The words were so simple. The idea was not unique. And yet, when he said it, you could feel the impact in the room. Derek had accurately linked his conjugal paranoia to his abandonment schema. If a defectiveness/shame schema was driving the jealousy, Derek's core belief could be stated as "I'll never be good enough for anyone."

And with his next words, Derek proved that was exactly his thought process with his girlfriend. "That's why I cheated. I wanted a spare if Tamika ever did leave. I hedged my bets so I'd never be without a girlfriend."

The defectiveness/shame schema led Derek to cheat as a way to prove to himself he was attractive, to improve his self-esteem. The more other women responded to him, the less he cared if Tamika might leave him, even if she had done nothing to suggest it.

But as we examined his violent episodes, abandonment regularly seemed like the trigger for physical abuse. Often in Derek's case, the physical aggression occurred in situations when Tamika wanted to go somewhere without him.

But this was not always the case. Each past incident of aggression was explored for the presence of schemas. Sometimes, Derek told us he got angry at Tamika even when she told him she loved him.

"I could never believe her. Whatever she did to show me she cared was never enough."

This response suggests a coexisting schema of emotional deprivation caused by emotional neglect during childhood.

The emotional deprivation life trap centers on fear, most clearly stated as "I'll never get the love I need." Emotional deprivation feels as if something is missing; there is an inner emptiness, a vague sense of needing something or someone to say, "Everything will be all right. You are safe."

Whenever a mother is in a violent relationship with her own partner, she is handicapped in her ability to adequately provide for her children's needs for comfort, safety, and affection. The abused mother is usually focused on appeasing her partner and preventing more violence; she has limited time and attention to devote to the children.

Each of Derek's adverse childhood experiences encouraged the development of different schema. Physical abuse equaled powerlessness; witnessing parental violence, defectiveness/shame; separation from his mother, abandonment and emotional neglect, emotional deprivation. In my experience, the mistrust/abuse schema accompanies every act of interpersonal violence.

"I know others will hurt me," Derek said, summarizing the schema perfectly. "I try to hurt them first."

After the early maladaptive schema have been identified and linked to adult abusive behavior, the next step is creating a new set of values and beliefs that will lead to intimacy and caring. Then comes the hard part: practicing the new world view and making it a part of one's identity.

The treatment process is called *self-change*. Derek substituted rational and balanced beliefs for his distorted reasoning. I believed that for Derek, the process was one of repentance. Derek was making himself a new person.

My use of the schema model is supported by research conducted by psychologist Donald Dutton, found in his clinical book, *The Abusive Personality: Violence and Control in Intimate Relationships*. Dutton found that wife assaulters showed systematic bias about their marital conflicts, corresponding to abandonment and a mistrust/abuse schema.

The study, directed by Dutton, was very complex and intricate. Dutton set up a series of experiments to "get inside the head" of the violent men in intimate relationships. Wife assaulters were compared to a group of happily married men, a group of men who were violent outside of their relationship and a group of men who experienced marital conflict but did not use physical violence to resolve the conflicts.

The study hired professional actors to play couples on videotape, in various conflict situations. In an abandonment scene, the wife told her husband that she was going on a long weekend trip to a nearby city, Seattle, with female friends. In a second scene, the schema was a fear of engulfment, getting too close in a relationship. In this situation, the woman complained to her husband that they did not share enough quality time. The third scene was neutral regarding changes in intimacy: the couple argued over how to spend their vacation together.

The wife assaulter group was the most prone to react to the conflict situations with anger, even more than the men whose violence was not relationship-specific. In keeping with this, the wife assaulter group also said more than the others that they would likely use violence to resolve the conflict if they had been in that situation.

The wife assaulters also tended to blame the wife for the conflict more than the other groups. The violent men perceived the man in the vignette as being personally humiliated by his wife's demands, while the nonviolent men barely saw them as demands.

Reaction to abandonment issues in the conflict situations also varied by group. Wife assaulters saw the videotaped conflicts relevant to their own relationships at a 78 percent level. Generally assaultive men related at a 54 percent level and maritally conflicted men at a 39 percent level, while the happily married men saw relevant abandonment issues only at a 29 percent level.

As I worked with Derek and other domestically violent men using a life trap curriculum, I found these offenders showed signs of five basic schema through which they misinterpreted their relationships: abandonment, defectiveness/shame, mistrust/abuse, powerlessness, and emotional deprivation.

Jeff Young's schema therapy model, the self-change process and especially my long-term experience with Derek, proved very helpful to me in developing a deeper understanding of how offenders made relationship decisions. But, alas, not all offenders had the same resources to address their issues.

CHAPTER 3

Sean and Disassociation

Usually, when an offender tells me that he does not remember his crime, that he was in an alcoholic blackout or has amnesia, I mark him down as a denier. He does not want to admit to the offense and is seen as refusing to take responsibility.

Then I met Sean. He told me he didn't remember viciously attacking, choking, and sadistically torturing his wife. I believed him. I didn't see his amnesia as an excuse. He really did not remember.

I first met Sean when he was a new inmate, transferred to Fox Lake Correctional Institution to serve his seven-year sentence, attain his GED degree, and to participate in sex offender and domestic violence treatment. I interviewed him for clinical monitoring due to his diagnosis of severe anxiety disorder. But I always ask about a client's offense, and Sean's story was fascinating.

When Sean first appeared in my office, he was the opposite of aggressive. Sean looked like the prototypical skinny, weak man on the beach who had suffered a bully throwing sand in his face. He was introverted and painfully shy. Even after we had worked together for six months, Sean never showed any anger, not even normal frustrations or minor irritations.

Sean was slight and emaciated. He was like a phantom, pale and with little definition. He walked in a slouch, hiding his face behind shoulder-length, thinning, grayish ash-blond hair. His harsh life and alcoholism made him look much older than his chronological age of fifty-five.

Sean's life before prison, before the violence, was similarly non-descript and bland. He dropped out of high school and supported himself with odd jobs for which he was paid under the table. He moved frequently and was in Florida when his mother got cancer, prompting him to return to his family home to take care of her.

Nothing in Sean's adolescent and adult history predicted his vicious crime. Sean took responsibility for his offense. Without protest, he identified himself as the person who committed the offense against his wife. He saw pictures of his wife with a black eye, a swollen and bleeding lip, and bruised body.

His response was, "I know I did this. I just don't remember."

Sean seemed as confused as anyone about his past history. He didn't appear to be the kind of person who could commit such horrendous acts of violence. When I asked, Sean had no clue why he would act in such an aggressive manner.

I thought it was possible that Sean might present a case of dissociative amnesia, a separation of consciousness from one's physical actions during the perpetration of a crime or other disturbing occurrence.

Dissociation is usually associated with childhood abuse. The traumatized child is faced with inescapable danger. He can't fight or run away, so he escapes into his mind. He separates his consciousness from his experience of being physically attacked or emotionally violated. It is a form of protection, enabling the child to leave the scene psychologically, to withdraw into his imagination.

Dissociation in adults frequently signals a significant exposure to childhood trauma. I had reviewed Sean's social service and psychological history in order to write my initial psychological report on him. There were no records to document any specific abuse.

But I felt there was a revelation to come because every time I tried to talk to Sean about his family, Sean shut down emotionally.

He regularly responded to these requests for more information on his past by telling me, "I don't want to speak bad about my mom or dad." Sean became agitated whenever I brought up the topic of his childhood. It seemed to be a minefield I couldn't cross.

But one day, while we were talking in my office, I asked Sean quite directly about his offense, "Do you remember anything about choking and sexually assaulting your wife, Vicky?"

Sean said, as he had before, "I don't remember that night." But then, he swallowed hard and with a look of pain in his eyes, murmured, "But I do remember choking another girlfriend when I was sober."

So the act of choking was not just limited to the experience he could not remember. I asked him, "Where did you get the idea of choking?"

Sean showed distress but answered my questions clearly and forcefully. "My father choked my mother and pulled her hair."

I know I looked shocked at this new assertion. Rather than waiting for my obvious follow-up question, Sean bravely continued, giving me the admission I had tried to get out of him for weeks. "My father beat me so much," he said, with an edge growing in his voice, "I couldn't go to school. I couldn't go to school because the bruises bled through my clothes."

He seemed angry for a moment, but then that quickly melted away. Sean's manner became frantic, fearful, like he had done something terrible and expected me to punish him. And then I saw signs of dissociation. His emotions went flat. I felt him reverting to a ghostly presence again.

Sean was dissociating in my office. I asked him simple, grounding questions to keep him in the present, to focus on things he could see, feel physically, or touch.

I told him, "Focus on how your body feels sitting in the chair. Stare at your hands and notice their outline." Then I gave him another task. "Name five things you can see in the room with you."

As he looked around and cited different objects, I thought to myself that I needed to learn more about dissociation. I wondered if dissociative amnesia might explain Sean's inability to remember committing his offense.

Dissociation is a mental process everyone uses at some time or to some degree and is extremely common. Examples include highway hypnosis, the act of letting your mind drift while still functionally driving on a highway. Dissociation can be useful when one visualizes being on an exotic beach while a dentist is drilling one of your teeth. Of course, dissociation can be slightly detrimental, such as being absorbed in a daydream during a boring business meeting and being asked a question you did not hear.

Dissociative disorders are a group of mental illnesses that involve a temporary detachment from reality rather than a psychosis, which denotes a complete separation from reality. When people experience an unpleasant situation and cannot fight or flee, they escape into their imaginations.

When faced with trauma and inescapable threat, dissociation is a self-protective mental process that develops spontaneously and becomes more practiced and automatic the more it is performed. The individual engaged in the dissociation feels numb, detached either physically or mentally and separated from the events as they are occurring.

In depersonalization, the individual feels a detachment or estrangement from a sense of self; it is the sensation of being an outside observer of one's mental processes or body, that is, feeling like one is in a dream. Some victims of this process have described feeling as if they were a machine or robot, acting without feelings. Others reported seeing themselves as playing a role in a movie. There may be a sense that you are watching yourself from behind your shoulder or from across the room.

A related experience is derealization, a sense that other people or the environment is unreal. In this scenario, the world may seem two dimensional or in some way dreamlike, such as an area that is veiled in a fog. During derealization, perceptual distortions occur, including changes in the size of objects or sounds seeming far away.

Dissociative amnesia involves gaps in memory, usually due to stressful or traumatic events. The memories still exist but are deeply buried within the person's mind and cannot be readily recalled. The memories may resurface later in life on their own or after being triggered by something in the person's surroundings.

Andrew Moskowitz explored the relationship between dissociation and violence in a 2004 article in the journal *Trauma, Violence and Abuse*.

Moskowitz noted that dissociative symptoms are at times experienced by the perpetrator during the commission of a crime. In a study, 15 percent of the respondents answered yes to this question: "Have you felt at times that, while being physically aggressive with your female partner, someone else was being aggressive with your victim and not you?"

Nine percent of the men stated they felt that they could actually see themselves from a distance being violent toward a female partner. And 24 percent answered that they felt changed, that they felt bigger or smaller, or that something else about them felt different.

Admissions of these dissociation symptoms and/or one's derealization (feeling as though the victim was not real) were often linked with both the frequency and severity of perpetrated violence. Men who reported dissociative experiences were more violent than men who did not.

Moskowitz cites a research project by E. Tanay, a forensic psychiatrist who studied fifty-three homicide offenders over a ten-year period and published the results in 1969. Tanay argued that 70 percent of these offenders had been in a dissociative state at the time of the crime. These offenders, who normally functioned well and had no history of psychiatric problems beyond some episodes of depression, shifted into an altered state of consciousness immediately prior to the crime.

Statistical studies found rates of pathological dissociation ranged from a low of 10.5 percent in a sample of violent men in a domestic violence treatment program to a high of 49 percent in a sample from a psychiatric hospital. Amnesia was at times reported after violent, premeditated crime and was frequently associated with alcohol and drug use and extreme emotional arousal.

Moskowitz speculated that the dissociative state allowed the individual to publicly express negative, unacceptable, and previously repressed aggressive or sexual impulses. Pent-up feelings of frustration or anger would thus be expressed explosively, since there was no socially acceptable outlet. Gaining distance from a normal sense of self allowed the perpetrator to act violently without personal shame.

Moskowitz also examined dissociation as the main mechanism for transmission of violence from one generation to the next, the so-called cycle of violence. Dissociation, in his view, is an adaptive response to childhood abuse. He identified a significant relationship between physical abuse history and the potential for dissociative and physical abuse.

One study involved women who were abused as children. Each woman's level of dissociation was assessed by the Dissociative Experiences Scale (DES). The DES consists of twenty-eight questions describing various kinds of dissociative experiences. These include missing parts of a conversation, finding evidence of doing things that they do not remember, or the experience of feeling that other people, objects, or the world around them are not real.

The women who abused their own children scored significantly higher on the DES than mothers who, despite having been abused as children, did not. The median DES score for the abusive mothers was 36, well over the cutoff of 30 usually considered indicative of severe dissociation. The median for non-abusing mothers was a score of 16. Dissociation, then, is something that significantly affects both male abuser and female victim alike.

My therapy contact with Sean did not allow me much time to explore either his childhood or his offense. I met with Sean weekly to help him manage a severe social anxiety disorder which was interfering with his ability to function in the regular prison population.

The prison population can, as an analogy, be described as filled with sharks ready to attack the weaker inmates. Sean, in a sense, was a guppy. As soon as he arrived at FLCI, a multidisciplinary team labeled him as vulnerable. Certain accommodations were made to help keep Sean safe. Instead of being given a cell with an inmate who might assault him or take advantage of him, Sean was what we referred to as "paired with care," and a minimally aggressive inmate was chosen as his cellmate.

Sean was so timid that he did not like eating in the chow hall, wary of the fifty men hustling about and shouting and abruptly sitting and standing to go. At FLCI, inmates could get a conduct report for not eating quickly enough. Because of his nervousness, Sean was allowed to eat early with the maintenance workers before the inmate crowd came in.

Our meetings became more frequent when Sean was taken off the academic waiting list and was assigned to start school. His guidance counselor, Mary, called me on the phone during his first visit. She wanted to know how to treat Sean, who in that moment was sitting in her office, shuddering, staring ahead, and not answering her questions about his preferences for his school schedule.

All Sean had told Mary was "I can't go to school" and "I won't go to school." If Sean refused to attend classes, it would result in punitive action, including being placed in segregation, where he would be locked in an enclosed cement room with nothing but a mattress and a toilet.

Mary sent Sean to my office, where I told him that he could not have a clinical excuse and would be expected to attend the two one-hour classes a day, one in remedial math and one in GED English.

Sean argued, claiming that his anxiety was too great for him to go to school. The school building at FLCI had a long hallway between the classrooms. In between classes, inmates crowded in the hallways and Sean thought he couldn't cope.

I gently explained to Sean, "It's important that you get your GED. Your guidance counselor, teachers, and I will help you manage your panic attacks."

The classes were small. There were four or five other students who worked independently with teachers, providing individual instruction.

The teachers allowed him to sit at the back of the class, next to the door and away from the other students. I made sure that he was told that in the event of an unmanageable panic attack, he could quietly leave the classroom.

When I met with Sean after these arrangements, his mood was quite changed. There was a little bit of confidence to be seen, especially when he told me, "I never ask to leave. But it helps my anxiety to know that I could if I wanted to."

He was pleased as he reported his use of relaxation skills in the classroom. "I took a few deep breaths and calmed down enough to work on my math assignment."

Sean looked like an entirely different person the day he attained his HSED, the high school equivalence degree. There was a ceremony for graduates in the prison gym. I attended and congratulated him on his achievement.

Sean became easier to work with. He smiled more, interacted with me more easily, answered questions with more than one word, and his posture became straighter and stronger.

As he got closer to release, Sean set up plans to move in with a sister, maintain sobriety, and live as independently as possible in the community.

Much progress had been made. His self-esteem was increased. He was better able to interact with inmates and teachers appropriately, and he had learned relaxation skills. Attaining his HSED suggested he was less of a recidivism risk.

As much as I wanted Sean to succeed on the outside, I was still not completely satisfied. No one at FLCI understood where all the rage that motivated his aggression came from. If Sean had truly dissociated during his offense, we needed to address this more explicitly. And I also believed that Sean needed to recover traumatic memories of his childhood and integrate them into a coherent sense of identity.

Helping Sean be a more confident individual was not enough. I wanted and needed to figure out how and why such a passive and compliant individual could turn into a raging and heinous batterer. The process of mere supportive counseling that I was doing was, in my opinion, not going to serve much of a purpose.

I believed that successful childhood trauma counseling needed to involve a lot of talking. Faith in the capacity of talk to resolve trauma dates back to Sigmund Freud, who in 1893 said, "Trauma immediately disappears when we had succeeded in bringing clearly to light the memory of the event by which it was provoked and in arousing its accompanying affect, and when the patient had described the event in the greatest possible detail and had put the affect into words."

In the schema therapy model, the client's task is to understand the childhood origins of his life traps. Trauma stories provide an explanation and a meaning for the abuse. Sean needed to understand intellectually that he was not to blame for the bad things that happened to him as a child and that his dysfunctional childhood molded his personality.

Each time I tried to approach Sean to discuss his traumatic childhood in our sessions, he withdrew and dissociated. I watched my words carefully so as to not suggest that I wanted him to reflect back on whatever kind of trauma he was trying so hard to forget. Sean's tolerance for discussing emotionally arousing subjects was zero.

But Sean thought revisiting his childhood meant that someone needed to take the blame for the abuse and neglect. He made it clear that he didn't want to blame his parents. "My parents had a terrible childhood themselves. They had financial problems and my mother was depressed." But Sean could not grasp that no matter how well-meaning his parents were, trauma-informed therapy focused on the reality of his childhood and the unalterable fact that his emotional needs were not met.

But Sean's memories of his childhood, whatever they were, evoked such a high arousal level that his ability to discuss them disappeared. I believed that to lower Sean's risk to reoffend was dependent on a full verbal analysis of his childhood and its effect on his offense. Yet Sean's tendency to dissociate when I even approached an intellectual analysis led to frustration and an urgency that I needed to attempted any discussion or exploration of childhood origins.

The ability to understand human behavior in terms of intentional mental states—that is, needs, desires, feelings, beliefs, goals, purposes, and reasons—is called metacognition or mentalization. These are the cognitive skills necessary for an individual to be successful in social interactions and gain an organized, coherent sense of self. Mentalization is thinking about thinking.

Peter Fonagy and Anthony Bateman, the editors of *Handbook of Mentalizing in Mental Health Practice*, define good mentalization skills as flexible and rational, using logic to solve emotional and social problems. Cognitive skills include using the scientific method of holding all factors constant and then varying one, inductive and deductive reasoning, examining perspectives of others, reflection, and abstract thinking.

Not everyone in general society gains full mentalization skills. Even when individuals are able to use deductive reasoning in their jobs like fixing a car's engine, many cannot apply these same skills to their emotional problems. Deficits include naïve realism, the over-valuation of one's own perspective, and the assumption that one's position is universally true and known to all others.

Developmentally, a child develops a theory of mind (ToM) around the age of two that allows him to understand that other people have thoughts, feelings, beliefs and motivations that differ from his. Without the ability to take another's perspective, the individual believes that everyone knows what the individual wants. With this assumption, failure to give that person what is desired is a willful act of maliciousness, rather than the result of a different point of view and alternative priorities.

Other forms of prementalization reasoning include psychic equivalence, which entails a lack of awareness of the relationship between internal and external reality. "What I think" becomes real and the guiding principle is "There are no possible alternatives."

Psychic equivalence is used by the stalker who is convinced that the celebrity he is harassing loves him, despite a restraining order. Another example is when a person feels sick, he or she might think that there is poison in his or her food. The hypothesis is that when a situation is dangerous, one's assumption has to be correct.

I wanted my therapy clients to talk about their perceptions and interpretations so that we could identify and correct the poor logic. I encouraged the client to speculate about others' motivations. For example, I might ask, "Why do you think she (or he) might be acting that way?"

Six months before Sean's release date, he was interviewed for participation in the FLCI Domestic Violence program, which was being facilitated by the social service department. Due to a staff shortage, the institution didn't have enough social workers, so an outside contract was given to Tamra Oman, an AODA (Alcohol and

Other Drug Abuse) counselor who came into the prison on Friday mornings to provide a twenty-four-hour session treatment program, using the life trap curriculum.

Tamra was an experienced clinician who also worked at Wisconsin's mental health institution for inmates, the Wisconsin Resource Center. Tamra was a unique therapist in that she was an adult survivor of childhood trauma (8 out of 10 ACES, Adverse Childhood Experiences). She was able to talk about healing childhood trauma from experience, not book learning.

Tamra was a large person with a large personality. Her enthusiasm and spirit were infectious. She had a contentment with herself despite struggles with her weight. She still fought to maintain sobriety from a drug addiction. At age forty-five, she suffered from a severe heart problem as a result of drug use. And she was a former inmate at the only Wisconsin state women's prison, in Taycheedah.

Sean responded wonderfully to working with Tamra. Most of the male offenders related to her, especially because she was ready to share her past indiscretions. "I was a victimizer as well as a victim," Tamra would tell the men. And she was able to promote the joy of making positive changes.

Tamra's treatment group was held in a small room with ten other group members and Tamra. Sean sat next to the door, always ready to leave if he felt a panic attack come on. But with Tamra's encouragement, he gradually began to share with the group and seemed to become more comfortable.

I shared my concerns about Sean with Tamra. I passed the group room on my way to get social services files and to go to the break room. I took every chance I could get to talk to Tamra. She was positive about my writings about life traps and said that the life trap model had helped her in her journey to change. She used my life trap curriculum in her treatment group for DV offenders.

It all spilled out of me one day. I noted my awareness of Sean's positive changes of increased self-esteem, better social skills, and ability to manage his emotions in a more productive way. However, the changes didn't assure me that Sean would never revert back to violence.

"Suppose once he's in the community, Sean continues feeling more confident and relaxed. He adapts a healthier lifestyle, even starts yoga or running, and does really well for a while. But then something bad happens," I speculated. "His sister dies or he encounters another obstacle. He stops yoga and slips into a depression. He starts drinking again. The life problem then triggers his tendency to dissociate, and it leads to violence in his relationship."

I believed that offenders needed to systematically conceptualize how their childhood affected their violence. I told her how reluctant Sean was in our individual session to discuss his childhood trauma. I asked Tamra if she thought offenders needed to intellectually understand the origin of the aggression. When an offender makes the connection cognitively, there is an aha moment, like a light going on inside of him

I asked her, "Is he learning to link his past with his current problems? Doesn't he need to get this insight in order to make sure he does not reoffend?"

Tamra responded by asking for me to be patient with Sean. She saw him progress. "I see him making the correlation, the connection, between the way he grew up and his problems today. He is gaining the understanding, you know, 'If my childhood had been different, I might have ended up differently. I'd probably be in a better place.'"

I sighed, worried still about Sean's future. "Why is the reflective process so hard, when the final understanding is so gratifying?"

"Because," Tamra answered, "if you start to question the basic beliefs that are the foundation of your life, your core schemas, there is an anxiety. You fear for your sense of self and stability in the world. Your defenses will be blown away. You feel naked, exposed, like a speck of dust in the wind that will be blown away and nothing will be left of you."

Tamra's voice and manner grew firm. "Sean has to go at his own pace. He needs to feel safe. It's like he is sitting on the shore of a frozen lake but is afraid to venture out. He's afraid the ice will break and he won't survive. But he sees me, his group therapist, someone who has already unpacked all the inner crap, examined the inside shit, and organized it. I'm out in the middle of the ice and I'm still standing.

"Sean sees the other group members out on the ice, some more fearful and closer to shore than others. Each of us is a symbol that he can be different. He can choose to be better. And no one had the right to tell him he didn't deserve to feel good."

I continued to see Sean until he left the prison. We worked together from 2008 to 2011. When he was released, he had already been approved for social security disability. He planned how he could exist in society, like going to Walmart only at night when the store was nearly empty.

Before he left FLCI, I talked to Sean about how it was okay to be angry. But this time, when he dissociated, he spoke in the most childish voice I had ever heard come out of a grown man. He sounded tiny, like a little boy who was being punished for being bad.

He cried out, "I never wanted to hurt anybody." I was devastated. In our three years together, it was Sean at his most vulnerable. He was reentering the community without the realizations he needed to defend himself. I told myself the system had served him as best as it could, but deep down, I still had serious doubts.

CHAPTER 4

George, Flashbacks and Hallucinations

George was a tall, big, burly thirty-two-year-old black man with a messy Afro and a scraggly beard. When he arrived at Fox Lake Correctional Institution, his preliminary investigative report listed his crimes as forgery, stealing a watch from his girlfriend's roommate, disorderly conduct, bail jumping, and possession of cocaine.

As a parole agent noted "each time he has been placed on supervision, he has absconded almost immediately, committed new crimes resulting in revocation."

To the Wisconsin Department of Corrections, George's case was not atypical. There were many offenders caught in a revolving door of crime and prison. The question that arose in my mind when treating prisoners like George was "Why doesn't the negative consequence of incarceration result in the offender stopping the behavior?"

George participated in an AODA (Alcohol and Other Drug Abuse) treatment program during one incarceration. Drug use had fueled much of his criminal activity. He also completed an anger management program and took vocational classes for making cabinetry.

While out of prison, he was involved in many reported acts of domestic violence. One of his victims had to go to a domestic violence shelter. She was in the process of a divorce from George and was afraid to leave the shelter for fear she would end up dead. George was arrested.

Some of George's crimes were particularly manipulative and conniving. One offense described George meeting a girl at a bar and joining her group of friends. The victim reported that George had bought her a drink that made her feel "fuzzy" and he then insisted on driving her car, since she could not drive safely. He then made sexual advances toward her that made her uncomfortable, so when they got to the next bar, she left quickly. The next day, she realized that her phone, bank card, and fifty dollars in cash were gone.

Another victim was an elderly and disabled man. This time, George entered his home, socialized with him, and prepared food in the kitchen. The polite old man finally found a way to ask George to leave, who did so, taking the old man's wallet with him.

Reading these details, George can be seen as a predator. He didn't care whom he hurt and picked vulnerable victims.

After being caught, George became a different person. When George was interviewed for the pre-sentence investigation report, the PSI, he actually asked to go to prison and his only other request was that he receive mental health treatment.

In a letter to the judge, George wrote that psychological help might help him "find out what is really wrong with me mentally, like why I can't sleep, why I cry so much, why I feel so alone and empty inside, and why I feel so confused and unloved."

George wrote an inmate request to be seen by psychological services immediately upon transfer to FLCI. I received his request the next morning. There was clear urgency in his declaration, "I need help!" I called security and asked that he be sent up to my office.

Despite the cruelty of his offenses and the desperation in his request for help, George seemed like another person when he came into my office. He said he was happy to be seen by a psychologist. He talked about himself with drama and irony, and surprisingly, he often made me laugh.

I was not expecting George to be funny. In introducing himself in my office that first afternoon, George mentioned his big head. I had not noticed any abnormality in the size of his head, but after he mentioned it, I started to see it his way. George made fun of himself and spent a few minutes delivering an entertaining riff about living with a big head and being teased for it.

But then George shifted and quickly settled into a description of the hell he was experiencing.

"I have constant memories," he admitted. "It's like opening a well of sewage." He reported flashbacks, intrusive memories, and nightmares. These symptoms form one of the categories of PTSD symptoms. It's referred to as reexperiencing the trauma, psychologically and physiologically.

George astounded me. He claimed to have three or four flashback episodes every day, which significantly disrupted his ability to function. Flashbacks are intense, extremely intrusive memories that feel as though the past trauma was being experienced in the present.

Describing a flashback he had experienced the day before, he said, "I was sitting in the chow hall eating my lunch while inmates around me were talking and laughing, stuffing their faces. Suddenly, I see my father in front of me, with his blue shirt and a crazy look on his face. I see him screaming, 'Goddamn you, boy, I am going to teach you a lesson you won't forget!'

"It comes out of nowhere, and then, *poof*, it's gone. I'll be back at the cafeteria table with my food in front of me and everyone staring at me. I never know when they are going to come, and sometimes, it seems like they go on forever. If I hadn't had one for a while, I can't enjoy it because I'm always fearful of the next attack."

George was a highly verbal and psychologically oriented inmate. He had already spent a good portion of his adult life trying to figure out what was wrong with him. He was very needy while in the middle of an emotional crisis. I spent two hours with George that afternoon. I saw him two to three times in the first few weeks and, after that, once or twice a week for the next nine months.

In addition to the individual therapy I would provide to help him deal with his frequent flashbacks and other PTSD symptoms, we needed to work on a release plan for his transition back into the community in a few short months.

As the first session drew to a close, George pondered his future. "The last times I was in prison, I just decided to get out and keep doing what I've always done: deal drugs, get into fights, start stealing and hustling for money."

George looked at me. I saw some hope in his eyes, but mostly, he projected surrender and despair.

George turned out to be the polar opposite of my client Sean. It was hard to wrench any information from Sean about his past. George's memories of his own childhood flooded out of him with urgency and emotional force. He often cried as he described disturbing memories of how his father beat his mother. He once became so agitated that I asked whether he might be too distressed to keep talking about the past.

He said, "I want to talk about it. I wouldn't have brought in up, if I didn't. I *need* to talk about it."

George lived with both his mother and father until age eleven. "My father worked as a correctional officer at the Milwaukee county jail. When he came home, he beat my mother. She was open game. Once, my father took a shotgun and cocked it against my mother's face like he was going to shoot it at her head." George confessed that his father had threatened to kill his mother numerous times, in numerous ways.

George's confessions, impossibly, seemed to get more horrifying as we continued our sessions. "He also beat my two older sisters," he told me, downtrodden. "They were around thirteen and fourteen years old when my mother finally left. My older sisters tried to protect me. May would hold me as we both had to listen to my father beating my mother on the other side of the wall. I'd wake up to my mother's scream that sounded like some raging animal attacking his prey. I remember standing in the doorway and watching my father rape my mother. I can't forget seeing the tears in her eyes. I wanted to help her but was too afraid of what would happen."

At this point in my interactions with George, I didn't think the suffering he went through could have been much worse. But I was wrong again.

"I was ten or eleven," George recalled. "Finally, I'd had enough and shouted to him, 'Leave her alone! She ain't did nothing!' My father made me sit on his lap and ordered me to say, "My mother is a bitch." He kept pinching me. He kept saying it over and over and saying it, and I went numb. Finally, I gave in and said it. I called her a bitch.

"I'll never forgive myself. She was so hurt. After that, she didn't look at me the same. I used to hang out with her, helping her cook. That all stopped after I called her a bitch. She said she didn't want to be around me anymore.

"Then I started taking the blame for anything that went wrong and then I was the target. Once, my father couldn't find his keys and was yelling that my mother must have taken them. I could see how afraid she was, so I said I'd been playing with them and they were under the couch. My father kicked me when I went to look under the couch. I lost my breath and hit my head on the floor. He found the keys in his work pants pocket.

"After my mother left, the first time, she took us kids with her but now she left on her own. Things got worse. My father would give my older sisters, ages thirteen and fourteen, alcohol and started going into their rooms at night. My sister Shelly was raped the most. Her first child, Faith, was my father's baby. She died when she was two."

I had heard many horrific stories from those I worked with in the prison system. Sadly, there was a continuum of violence in childhood stories. But what George was telling me was one of the worst things I had ever heard. Outwardly, I listened compassionately. Inside, I was stunned by the ongoing horror and degradation of his past.

"Finally, my mother came back with a man they called Charlie Brown," George told me, and here, I hoped that his misery had come to an end. It was not to be. "And all of us were to live with her. We thought things would be better, but it didn't. We were just a check to her every month. She gave us each thirty dollars and told us that was all we would get each month. She spent the rest on beer and drugs. We would have to watch her get high and play cards while we were hungry.

"I was twelve years old, now physically confronting Charlie Brown when he abused my mother or sisters. After I hit him for hitting my sister Opal, he told my mom that he didn't want me in the apartment and made me sleep in the basement. I had fixed it up like a cool man cave, although it was cold in the winter. Then I got to know the white lady, Brenda, who moved in next to my mother. They became friends, and Brenda told me I didn't have to live in the basement anymore.

"She wanted me to sleep in her bed and screw her. So I did. I had a good deal, though. She gave me food and a warm place to sleep. She bought me nice clothes, alcohol, and drugs. I got to bring my guys to her place and party. I was the big man in town."

There had been many shocking aspects to his past. But when he seemed proud about his sexual relationship with Brenda, I had to interrupt him. "You were twelve years old. You were sexually assaulted."

George didn't see himself as victimized by Brenda. He liked the lifestyle. "I got what I wanted," he said. He grinned and pantomimed being a guy who was self-confident and whom people respected.

"But did you want to have sex with her? Was it really your choice?" I asked. "What did this woman look like?"

Here, George's act of being cool and sexy came to an abrupt halt. "Brenda was the same age as my mother. Fat and ugly. I had to be on drugs to fuck her. No, I did it because that was my job. I certainly enjoyed the cool clothes, alcohol, and drugs."

There was no question in my mind that what he had been involved with was, despite its nonviolence, sexual assault, and we had to process it. I helped George explore the negative effects of his arrangement with Brenda. "Physical love," I told him, "is not meant to be a business arrangement." I explained what psychology tells us about how a sexual assault might negatively affect a preteen. Any boy, age twelve, who had the same experience would have confused thoughts and feelings. We discussed how his relationship with Brenda might have led him to develop a coarse and hardened attitude toward women.

George digested that information. Then he said sadly, "My mother said that Brenda was my foster mom. But everyone knew my mom had pawned me off. She knew what Brenda wanted me for. I think she may have been part of the deal because I know Brenda gave her money."

George seemed defeated. I asked him what he was thinking. It was another memory.

"When I was seventeen, I got caught stealing and was sent to a boy's home. When I got back, I used crack cocaine for the first time with my mother. She'd kiss my head and I felt loved. I haven't stopped using since."

As a potential high school dropout, George had a chance at redemption. "I was put in this program, kind of an internship at the University of Wisconsin Hospital. I washed the dishes in the kitchen, but during my shift, the dieticians spent time with me. They taught me stuff and said I should go on to technical college and become a dietician."

I felt my spirits lift a little inside as George told me this story. Obviously, I was heartened to hear about any community intervention program that encouraged high risk youth to think beyond the streets. A kid like George would have been desperate for some positive role models. I visualized George, a bright, energetic teenager, working in the hospital, gaining encouragement from those who wanted to him to have a chance in life.

Then George said, "I quit the program."

Without knowing George's mental health challenges, one could assume that George quit because he was lazy, so unwilling to work to better himself that he refused the help of others. In reality, the reason George quit was not out of laziness or a lack of caring. He quit because of his past.

"The women reminded me of Brenda," George said softly. "I kept thinking they wanted me for sex. I'd hear them talk about me behind my back. They'd mumble words like *penis* or ask me to show them my dick. After that I never could keep a job. I'd get drunk the night before work and call in sick. I'd keep hearing my coworkers talking about me saying, 'Look at that lowlife. Just like his daddy said, he won't be nothing. He should be ashamed of himself.'"

I asked George, "But you know that the women weren't saying those things, don't you? You know that nobody was really talking about you. Right?"

He looked at me, and without flinching or changing his tone of voice, he stated simply, "I know what I hear."

George did not fully realize it, but he was informing me that he had experienced auditory hallucinations. Hearing voices is usually associated with psychosis, a complete breakdown from reality. But he showed no other signs of a psychotic disorder. This was a complex situation for me as a psychologist because when men are pretending to act crazy in prison, "I hear voices" is the number one symptom reported. I had to consider that George might have been acting psychotic for a private reason.

But deep down, I didn't doubt him. And I didn't believe he was psychotic. Hallucinations are a symptom of complex posttraumatic stress disorder and a sign of extreme early trauma. George was distorting reality. He heard voices no one else heard. But the voices were from his past. They were more accurately flashbacks to past experiences of his parents or teachers putting him down, yelling at him, making him feel worthless.

George admitted that these flashback experiences interfered with his ability to function. He said, "I can read a book and be on page 249 but not remember what I was reading. I did a page of fractions but then forgot everything on the quiz."

George struggled to describe his experience of the flashbacks. "They seem to come out of nowhere. It's like reliving a video. I see the movie being projected on the screen but can hear and feel what is happening. I'm *in* the movie. I see my father coming at me with his open hand and can feel the slap on my face.

"I know I'm in your office or in my cell at the same time the flashback is occurring, and in the back of my mind, I tell myself, 'This isn't real.' But the video image of the past pulls me in. I'm stuck until the scene completes itself. If I interrupt it, my next flashback will pick up on the moment I had first paused the action."

The term *flashback* defines a psychological phenomenon in which an individual has a sudden, involuntary, and usually powerful reliving of a past experience. It is a type of dissociative experience. Conscious awareness is hijacked by images, feelings, and sounds from the past so vivid and with emotions so intense that the individual is unable to recognize it as a memory, rather than something that is happening in real time.

The neurological experience involved in a flashback is described by Bessel Van der Kolk in his book *The Body Keeps the Score: Brain, Mind, and Body in the Healing of Trauma.* He discussed how, on a brain scan, individuals who experienced flashbacks showed abnormal brain patterns. The biggest area of brain activation was in the right lower center of the brain, which is the limbic system, the emotional brain. The limbic system operates only in terms of survival with limited behavioral options: fight/flight/freeze.

Van der Kolk also indicated that trauma deactivates Broca's area, the language center in the brain. Simultaneously, cognitive processes go offline, including the ability to sequence events, identify cause and effect, grasp the long-term effects of our actions, or create coherent plans for the future.

Broca's area is the region of the brain that allows the person to put thoughts and feelings into words, to self-reflect, have a feeling of cohesion in the moment, and experience continuity through time.

Mental time travel is the ability of the human mind to have a sense of recollection of self at a particular time in the past, a sense of awareness of the self in the lived present, and to project the self into the imagined future. This awareness of time and sequence first becomes apparent in major shifts during the ages of two and five. The capacity to reflect on the self across time and to integrate temporal changes is disrupted during the flashback experience. In essence, time becomes jumbled.

Talking about his past increased George's frequency and intensity of his flashbacks. Unfortunately, this is a common response to processing traumatic memories in therapy. Symptoms sometimes get worse before they get better. But it pained me to know that for George, the nature of the memories was not changing over time nor were his emotional responses diminishing. Each flashback seemed to retraumatize him.

I remember how George would stare straight ahead in my office, experiencing a horror so great he could not put it into words. As he experienced the flashback, I often repeated quietly, insistently, "This is a memory. It isn't happening now. You are remembering something that happened in the past. It's not happening now. You are safe now."

I hoped, with this process, that my verbalizing might stimulate George's language center, orient him to the present, allow him to distance himself from the memory, and gain a sense of himself as an adult, no longer the fearful child.

The institution psychiatrist provided different psychotropic medications to see if any might help him with George's PTSD symptoms. None seemed to make any positive difference. Instead, the meds all gave him varied negative side effects, from hyperactivity all the way to total lack of energy and motivation. Sometimes, George said the medication made him feel worse. George was frustrated, and I felt upset that we were not helping him.

In sessions, I coaxed and gently prodded George to try new psychological interventions to lower his anxiety level. He was open with his opinions. He disliked a guided imagery script I used, asking him to visualize containers for his anxiety, but he was able to use safe place imagery to help him deal with the anxiety which always preceded a flashback.

My favorite relaxation skill to teach is mindful meditation. To me, mindful meditation was an all-around cure for whatever ailed you. The practice helped the client develop the skill to be in the moment. The mission was to forget the past and ignore the future.

Often, when meeting with inmates who complained of high levels of arousal, I played a nine-minute CD. A women's voice guided the listener in the skill of focusing on one's breath and paying attention to the present moment. I thought it was particularly valuable when the female speaker said, "Thoughts will pop up. But imagine the thought like a twig running down a stream and floating away."

Every inmate who listened to the compact disc enjoyed the sense of calm gained in this focus on the breath. Right away, though, I saw how difficult it was for George to shut his eyes and remain still. I could see him trying to listen, but his body seemed almost to spasm. He moved uncomfortably in his chair. The expression on his face suggested agony.

It was clearly was not working. I shut the CD off. George opened his eyes and said with an air of failure, "I had visions of choking my father. I couldn't stop the images in my head."

George was not able to handle this basic, fundamental skill of self-soothing. It was as if George was in a track and field event and was the only runner wearing chains. I promised him he would eventually feel better and find the ability to do self-relaxation. But as I learned more about his past, in the sessions that followed, I began to have my doubts.

The most difficult memories for George, I learned, were of his father sexually assaulting him in his bed at night. The flashbacks were vivid and visceral. He told me he could sense his father's breath from behind his ear. He could hear his father's grunting. George admitted with shame that some memories he could not share with me.

These memories had a damaging effect beyond George hating himself. They prevented George from a relationship with his two young sons.

George had decided that he could not live with his sons for fear of repeating the horrible acts his father had done to him. He had read the statistics. He believed he was bound to eventually become his father.

George talked gently about these boys and his self-perceived inadequacies as a father. The worst day for him had been when the boys, ages four and six, left with their mother to move to Tennessee. He was amicable with his ex-wife. She had divorced him, not due to any violence but because of his drinking and difficulties with commitment. After that, George mostly communicated with his sons over the phone.

George told me he was haunted by the image of his youngest son's face on the day they left.

"My younger boy, Elias, would climb into my lap, affectionate like any normal kid, wanting to be hugged. I wanted to hold him close but touching him felt perverted. I'd see my father's face and felt his tongue in my mouth and feel sick. I remember pushing him away, telling him to go play with his brother. I could feel his disappointment and felt like shit for not giving him the love he deserved."

This emotional struggle was seemingly endless for George, navigating between wanting to be close and then being afraid of the intimacy. Implicit memories of abuse blocked and frustrated him.

"Sometimes when I was with the boys, I'd feel a surge of anger. I'd be trying to enjoy a nice outing, like a barbecue, sitting quietly with my boys. I'd suddenly feel angry and have an impulse to slap their faces. I'd see myself in my mind slapping them, and the picture seemed so real, as if I had already done it. I'd have to get away. I was afraid of what I might do to them."

Perhaps some people think that psychologists are always in control of their emotions when dealing with their clients. Sometimes, what happens on the inside is very different from what is shown on the outside. I felt deep anger toward George's father for forcing his son to undergo such horror that it interfered with George's ability to bond with his own sons.

Despite how honest and forthcoming George had been with me about his past, I noticed that his revelations did not help his inability to sequence time. He was still having issues distinguishing what was in the past and separating it from the present and the future.

When George's release date was six weeks away, he still did not have any housing set up for himself. George's two older sisters lived in Milwaukee. His parole officer had already asked George if staying with one of them was an option.

George was adamant. "I won't stay with either of them. Not going to happen."

The alternative was extremely negative: a halfway house in the most drug-infested part of the city.

I argued with him, trying to show George the logic of staying with a family member. These discussions often got heated. The results were always the same. I tried to keep George calm enough to make a good decision, but he always became too upset.

I told him that his living with a sister, if one accepted him and the placement was approved, would be a smart choice. His sisters had no known criminal records, and statistics suggested that living with a family member greatly increased the chances of an offender's successful reintegration into society.

I also reminded him that his memories of his sisters, especially June, his second oldest, were generally positive. He had described their efforts to protect him from his father's displeasure or comforting him after an abusive incident.

So I asked George, "Why wouldn't you want to live with one of your sisters if they gave approval? It wouldn't be forever, just until you got a job and your own place. What's so bad about living with them?"

To answer this question, George told me about his last family interaction two years ago at Christmas.

George described a warm welcome. "Everyone made such a big fuss that I was there. I played with my nieces and nephews and everyone got along. June convinced me to spend the night. They had planned a big event the next day."

Then he said, "I left before anyone got up in the morning."

I almost shouted at him. My voice rose without my being able to modulate it. "Why? Why wouldn't you stay? It sounds lovely." I imagined his sister finding him gone in the morning and could see her disappointment in my mind, knowing she would likely not see him again for another few years.

George described his sisters as intrusive, violating his personal space. "They want me to talk to them. They're always asking me, 'How are you? How do you feel?' They smother me."

"They just want to love you." I said. "You could be assertive and tell them that you feel smothered. If you asked them to give you a little space, you would stay longer."

And then George revealed the real reason he did not stay longer with his family at Christmas. It was an explanation that was difficult for me to counter. "When I see my sisters, I remember them having to watch my abuse. I see pity and shame in their eyes. My sisters remind me too much of the past."

No matter how hard I tried to convince him that his sisters had only love and compassion for him, George would not change his mind. His sisters, whom he had once loved, now represented a relationship triggering shame.

I usually recommend that an offender seek out counseling in the community, once released. But for George, I had to go a step further. County services were limited in Milwaukee, and there was a long waiting list of those requesting therapy. George would be leaving the institution without much money or any medical insurance.

Psychological services for the Department of Corrections in Wisconsin hired both institutional and community psychologists. The community psychologists usually performed evaluations to help the court determine sentencing. There was little time for ongoing therapy. However, I knew the supervisor of the Milwaukee region community psychologists, Erica. When I called her, she readily agreed to take over George's therapy after his release.

For any therapy client, transitioning from one psychologist to another is an emotionally wrenching event that needs to be processed. George resisted seeing a new psychologist because he didn't know if he could trust him or her.

George did not have a good attitude toward psychologists in general, once telling me, "They don't care. They're nosy and laugh about my problems at the dinner table."

Due to George's uneasiness, I arranged a conference call with Erica so he could hear her voice and perceive her genuine interest in helping him. This did help. George and I then continued to process his feelings until he left the prison.

I called George up to my office the day before he was to leave, in order to reduce his anxiety as much as possible. I felt no longer like a psychologist but a life coach. "You can do it. You can adjust to a halfway house and follow the rules. You can work with Erica, learn more about yourself, and maybe find some medication that would ease the depression, cure the PTSD symptoms, and make the effects of early trauma nonexistent."

George left Fox Lake Prison the next day, at eight o'clock on a Tuesday morning in August. His parole officer from Milwaukee picked him up and dropped him off at his assigned housing. George would then report to this officer the next day.

It is a fair and difficult question as to whether I was optimistic about George's success outside of prison. I think I am an optimist in general. I think I had to be, in order to do the work with offenders as I did for so many years. But I knew on that August morning that George was not ready to leave me.

Two weeks went by before I had time to check in with Erica. I was hoping to hear that George was receptive to working with her.

Instead, Erica said, "George absconded as soon as he was dropped off at the halfway house. He left supervision, and no one has heard from him since. He never even gave me the chance to meet him."

As I wrote this chapter on George, he was still marked on the Wisconsin offender registry website, on absconder status. I expected that George would do his best to stay off the grid. He was not likely to ask for mental health assistance from the Wisconsin Department of Corrections.

One of my fears is that George, either slowly or perhaps very quickly, developed a hard shell around himself, numbed his feelings with substances, or transformed back into the slick manipulator who was described in his criminal records. The other possibility was no better. George, burdened with the guilt and shame we had brought to the surface in our sessions, might have committed suicide so that he no longer could hurt anyone anymore.

CHAPTER 5

Jake and the Difficulty of Change

Jake was scary in appearance. It was fair to say that he would inspire fear if you met him on a dark, empty street. His face was set in an expression the inmates call *mean-mugging*. It warned everyone not to mess with him. A strong, well-muscled street fighter type, at twenty-eight, Jake looked like a man in control. His basic creed could be summed up as "my way or the highway."

But in front of authority, Jake was deferential, smooth, and superficially charming. I knew Jake through the domestic violence treatment program. I was Jake's teacher, his group facilitator, the person who could decide his fate, at least for the next two years. I was an object he wanted to manipulate.

Before 2001, when Wisconsin passed a "truth in sentencing" law, designed to force inmates to serve their entire sentence, a parole system was set up to offer the inmates time off for good behavior. An inmate became eligible for early release after serving a certain portion of the sentence, completion of a recommended treatment program, and consistent good behavior. With successful completion of the four-month group, Jake could be considered by a parole board, assigned by the governor, for early release. Completing treatment was generally believed to lower an offender's risk to commit a new offense and made him less of a danger to society.

Jake was serving a twenty-year sentence for aggravated battery and attempted murder, involving a vicious attack on his wife in a bus station parking lot. Jake was at a high risk for recidivism. He had a history of two assaults on a previous wife and an assault in a bar, which in the latter case resulted in serious harm. He was recommended for a domestic violence program, but there were not high expectations for him.

Jake needed to pass the domestic violence program or he would be stuck at FLCI's medium-security facility until a mandatory release date eighteen months in the future. Successful completion of his DV requirement would allow him to be considered for transfer to a less restrictive prison.

Jake claimed he was highly motivated to attend weekly group meetings, complete homework assignments, and write a relapse prevention plan, which anticipated high-risk situations that might trigger an urge to use violence and identified ways to cope with those urges.

Don, a male social worker, and I were in charge of running the DV treatment program at FLCI. Our job was to interview Jake and other inmates on the waiting list as part of a screening process before anyone entered our group.

Jake could not start treatment until he convinced his treatment providers, Don and me, that he took responsibility for his violence and admitted he wanted it to stop.

My co-facilitator and I interviewed each candidate in my office. We had ten to twenty minutes with each inmate to assess their readiness to change.

Don and I had already read Jake's social services file which provided details about his offense history.

One of the first things said to these offenders in meetings was the most important phrase: "Describe your offense." The court had found him guilty. First of all, he had to accept his guilt. It was no use providing treatment if Jake could not admit that he did anything wrong. This was a crucial first step. The self-change process involved looking at the thoughts leading to the offense, identifying how they were distorted, and then changing the thoughts. Once Jake no longer denied the act, the curriculum would address denial of intent and denial of harm. Excuses were challenged: i.e., "I didn't mean to hurt her" or "She fell down, I didn't push her" or "She was white and bruised easily."

The *readiness to change* concept was developed when James Prochaska and Carlos DiClemente, professors at Rhode Island University in 1977, were hired by the tobacco industry to research the problem of nicotine addiction. Why did so many people have such difficulty changing their smoking habit?

Prochaska and DiClemente studied men and women from the general public who were able to successfully quit smoking. The researchers found that the psychological process of intentionally changing behavior followed a series of five stages in the decision-making process.

Research was expanded to study recovering alcoholics who were able to maintain sobriety for five years. Individuals addicted to drugs, gambling, and overeating were also studied. The results generally related to any intentional change process. Those trying to diet, stop smoking, maintain sobriety, or stop gambling or overeating went through similar stages.

Successful subjects demonstrated the same stage progression whether they used religion, behavioral or humanistic psychotherapy, or simply stopped "cold turkey." Prochaska and DiClemente published their findings in a popular book called *Changing for Good* in 1983.

The first stage occurs before the individual makes a decision to change. It is called *precontemplation* (not ready). The attitude of "I don't have a problem" prevents the change process from even starting. Individuals in this stage do not see themselves as the cause of the problem. They blame everyone else. There is no desire to change.

The second stage is *contemplation* (getting ready). In this stage, the individual thinks, "Maybe I have a problem," and is open to hearing about others who have succeeded in overcoming their specific addictions. In contemplation, the person might consider the pros and cons of changing his or her behavior but remains ambivalent. The immediate gratification gained from the problem behavior outweighs the future goal. For example, the pleasure of eating dessert regularly is stronger than the wish to look good in a bathing suit.

In the third stage, preparation, the person is considering change, such as going on a diet or stopping using drugs within the next six months. The individual needs to make a plan for success, or without a plan, he or she will fail. For example, an alcoholic might stop going to bars but does not plan how to deal with being offered alcohol in some other social setting.

Treatment involves the client participating in the preparation stage, actively making a plan to change, and starting the action stage. Maintenance is the last stage when the individual continues the plan until it becomes part of his or her daily life.

Jake said that he wanted to change. He was asked to describe his assault on his wife, Melanie, in the parking lot of a bus station.

"Melanie didn't return home on the bus, after I sent her a ticket to come home from her mother's. She called me to pick her up the next day. As soon as I saw her, I started punching her and didn't stop until some people standing by held me back and called the police."

Jake had admitted to us that he committed the assault. But he seemed to believe Melanie deserved it because she didn't arrive home when he had told her to.

"She knew I wanted her home," he rationalized. "She was asking for it."

Don and I stared at him, surprised, despite the shocking stories we had heard. Usually, the inmates were not so open about their anti-social beliefs. Jake saw our reaction and quickly tried to walk back his statement.

He knew what treatment staff wanted him to say, and that was the next thing out of his mouth: "I am sorry about my violence and want to stop." He knew we didn't believe him, but Jake also was savvy enough to recognize that if he said the right words, we would be obligated to put him in the group. His words were documented in our report. I had no proof about whether his intentions were real or not.

So Don and I accepted him into the domestic violence group. We sent a list of participating inmates to the social workers and security with the times and dates, which were on each Wednesday.

The parole commissioner arranged a hearing for the month after Jake was scheduled to complete the program. After the program ended, I would have the responsibility to write a report on Jake's program participation and progress. Jake wanted to go to minimum custody where he could get work release and make some money before reentering society. But if I indicated he had not made enough progress in the group, Jake would be forced to stay at FLCI until his release.

Jake knew all this. He said all the right things. It was impossible to be certain at that point if his motivation was internal, i.e., was truly a desire to change because he wanted to stop hurting other people. He still seemed to be in the precontemplation stage. He didn't think violence was absolutely wrong. He did not define his aggression as a problem. He did not feel bad (shame) about his behavior.

Don and I learned fairly early in the process that Jake did not believe he was the root cause of his problem. His view was that others were just as abusive as him; unfortunately, he was the one who got caught.

"I had thoughts of her," he said of Melanie, "probably messing around with another man. The only thing I was feeling was to hurt her for making me feel the way I did, which was feeling hurt. I was feeling as though she had lied to me and one way or other, I was going to get even with her. Even if I would have killed her, I didn't care. That's just the way I was feeling, like I had been betrayed or used.

"I knew she would screw me over. Every woman I've known has cheated, even my mother. This started at a young age for me, something that I've always believed. Being cheated on and feeling the emotional pain and hurt was not for me. If she hurts me, then I'll hurt her physically." He paused, considering what he had just said. "Mentally anyway," he added.

We had already discussed the concept of life traps, and the inmates were familiar with the term and its categories. I asked Jake what life traps he felt applied to him.

"My life trap was mistrust/abuse. I couldn't trust anyone. Also, the powerlessness life trap. Controlling women is a belief of mine. If you are not in control, then you're weak."

"How about defectiveness?" another group member asked.

Jake turned to his fellow inmate and shook his head. "No, I never felt bad about myself a day in my life. I'm the man." He laughed. No one else joined him in the room.

Jake frequently told others how great he was. He was his own public relations firm. This quality resulted in other inmates generally shunning his company. No one really liked Jake. He was not an easy guy to like.

Jake acted as if he was better than anyone else, especially women. He clearly resented that as a woman, I was an authority figure in the prison. He was forced to comply with my directions. I could see him stiffen when I gave him feedback or reminded him of a late assignment. Jake would squirm visibly when I gave direction to my co-therapist, Don. The fact that Don, as a man, listened to me as the lead facilitator, but that I was also a woman contradicted everything Jake believed.

Most inmates in group learned something from the respectful relationship between a male therapist and a female therapist. But Jake showed disgust. His deference to me was forced and disingenuous. Don agreed with me that Jake believed that despite my experience and position, he could manipulate me.

In fact, I was not worried about being conned by Jake. But I did want to help him and it seemed very unlikely I could. I saw little genuine emotion in Jake's interactions in the group. His feelings seemed superficial. He had no problem talking about feeling betrayed and used by Melanie. But when I tried to explore in a deeper way the feelings inside him, all Jake could do was talk about his anger. The emotions under the anger, like hurt or vulnerability, never quite reached the surface.

One day, Jake surprisingly stated a rational, balanced counterstatement to his previously expressed beliefs. "I cannot control Melanie," he said aloud. "She has the right to do what she wants. I'm her husband, not her boss."

But shortly thereafter, Jake stood out in the group by his frequent, impulsive sexist jokes about women. It contradicted his previous insight, suggesting, "I can control Melanie. Men have privileges. Women cannot be trusted."

Don and I asked Jake to stop making the sexist jokes that amused only him. The other men soon got tired of hearing them and responded negatively, but Jake continued.

At the end of the session, I gave him a special assignment: Write down your old beliefs and then your new ones.

Despite his punctuation and grammar, Jake did some positive soul-searching. He wrote, "A lot of men see women's as sex objects. I know this because I am one. And since the beginning of time, men has to have them all. Black men's grew up seeing their big brothers, uncle, and male cousins, with all kinds of women…We were also taught that if your women looks good, there will always be someone out there standing and waiting. So don't have men's in your house when you're not home."

Jake titled the next part of his assignment "Alternative Situations." He stated in part, "It is her house as well as mine, and she have the right to have over whomever she pleases. And I should believe and trust the woman whom I share a home with."

I wanted to believe Jake's new humanistic and compassionate vision of relationships. From his verbalizations, it appeared he had learned something. He eventually stopped interrupting class with the sexist jokes. Maybe it was a sign that he no longer held those sexist attitudes.

Alternatively, though, perhaps Jake had finally learned that sexist remarks were a threat to his objective to pass the class. I couldn't tell whether Jake was just playing a game or was being genuine in his efforts to learn how to develop and maintain a new, equal, and caring relationship style.

In the group, Jake heard many different reasons to change. One reason I provided was very much of interest to Jake: good sex. Questionnaires distributed in different countries, including the United States, England, Italy, and Denmark, had shown that a majority of men and women associated equality of power in relationships with more enjoyable sex. Among all the things said in the group, this was the thing that seemed to make the most impact on Jake.

I don't usually obsess so much about an offender's manipulation. But Jake always seemed to be carefully measuring my response to him. Superficial charm can be a sign of psychopathy, a condition without conscience or remorse, a mixture of the criminal and the narcissistic. One study found that psychopaths get worse with treatment.

Research with batterers found there are three different kinds of DV offenders: overcontrolled, emotionally volatile, and generally violent.

Donald Dutton proposed this trimodal view of assaulters of women and summarized his research supporting his theories in *The Abusive Personality: Violence and Control in Intimate Relationships.*

Overcontrolled batterers are defined by a limited criminal history, usually Operating While Intoxicated or OWIs, as it is called in Wisconsin. They are usually aggressive only in a family setting, have a positive social attitude and a passive personality. Alcohol use overlaps with the violence. Inmates in this category are usually very pleasant and score high on social desirability scales.

The emotionally volatile DV offender's violence is impulsive and undercontrolled. Mood swings are extreme and the relationship feels like a roller coaster. I find this type of DV offender is usually motivated to get treatment because the high level of distress comes back regularly and the offender is interested in learning emotional management skills.

Jake definitely fit into the third category, that of the generally violent. This type of offender is aggressive both in and out of the family. In research, generally violent men score low in empathy, use violence as an instrument to obtain a secondary goal, and report high levels of physical violence during childhood. And despite acting in an emotionally aggressive way, these men remained inwardly calm.

Neil Jacobson, in the early 1990s, as cited in Dutton's book, studied a sample of severely violent men. Their heart rates and other psychophysiological responses were monitored while they argued with their partners in a laboratory conflict.

The autonomic response of a human to a conflict, threat, or danger involves an increase in arousal and heart rate, otherwise known as the fight/flight response. Generally violent men showed a heart rate decrease while they argued. This type of offender showed the highest levels of violence, did not need alcohol to be aggressive, was the most criminally oriented and used violence instrumentally. They committed crimes methodically and without emotion.

Jacobson called generally violent men "cobras." Emotionally volatile men were "pitbulls." More recent research has questioned both Dutton's trimodal model and the sharp distinction between men who are impulsive and men who use instrumental violence.

But clinically, I found the three distinct types of domestically violent men fairly clear. Assigning the category of generally violent offender to Jake allowed me to understand him better and help in predicting his future behavior.

A generally violent type of offender is associated with predominant mistrust/abuse schemas. Jake easily identified mistrust/abuse and powerlessness leading him to trust no one, not even his intimate partner. Jake was raised in a family with violence and grew up in a gang-infested Chicago housing project. Life was a battle with no one on his side.

In relationships, the memory of being abused and a sense of threat are triggered when other people are physically and emotionally close. The generally violent offender is not able to let down his armor and trust because he never experienced the comfort and safety gained in close relationships. Intimacy is not possible without trust.

The generally violent offender seemed to have no shame. The nature of shame is explored in Michael Lewis's *Shame: The Exposed Self.* Lewis described shame as a negative self-evaluation, the conscious awareness of the self as reflected through another person's eyes. It is a global negative evaluation of the self. The shame is not produced by a specific situation but by the individual's interpretation of a situation.

"The phenomenological experience of the person having shame," Lewis explained, "is that of a wish to hide, disappear or die ... The physical action accompanying shame includes a shrinking of the body, rising heat in the face, blushing, and averted gaze."

With guilt, the individual accepts blame for a problem but sees it as a specific mistake. Shame-sensitive individuals view mistakes as an indication of a general flaw in themselves. The error or failure is considered a reflection of self-worth.

Instead of representing the thought "I did something bad," shame equals "I am bad." Guilt can motivate the self to change; in shame, however, our consciousness is filled with a self that is of no value and not worth anything, broken and ready to be tossed away.

Lewis went on to write, "The emotional state (of shame) is so intense and has such a devastating effect of the self-system that individuals presented with such a state must attempt to rid themselves of it."

Narcissism effectively acts as a mental mechanism to bypass the shame and to avoid the negative affective experience. The narcissist steers clear of self-reflection and rigidly adheres to rules about how people should or shouldn't act. Any failure is not his/her fault; he or she either blames others and/or unrealistically claims the failure as a success.

Jake's profile also included a high level of narcissism. In the life trap materials I provided the inmates, narcissism was listed as a counterattack for the defectiveness/shame schema. Jake, of course, made no progress there as he always denied that he had ever felt defective, inferior, inadequate, or less important than anyone else.

I described the schema of defectiveness/shame to the offenders in our group as a continuum, ranging from an extremely negative evaluation to an extremely positive one. On one end is the unworthy part of the schema, in the middle is a balanced belief in one's value, and at the other end, an extreme belief in entitlement.

"It's an all-or-nothing seesaw," I explained. "If you are not perfect, then you are completely flawed. On one end, you feel hyperpositive. On the other side, you're in a pond full of scum."

Most of the group members nodded and laughed. They were able to remember moments feeling like a zero and were able to relax and get in touch with it. Moments in the group like that one were so important. It helped the offenders trust enough to share vulnerable feelings and know that they were not alone.

But I could see by looking at Jake that he was shut off and not paying attention. I decided to push him a bit emotionally. I asked him directly, "Do you ever feel defective, no good, worthless, and unlovable?"

"I can't really relate to it," Jake responded. He looked at everyone in the group and knew they expected him to admit to this common negative emotion. I felt certain that all the other inmates knew that Jake was surviving by pushing the negative self-evaluation away.

"Maybe a small part of me," Jake said, making an effort to connect to the issue of self-worth. "I hate when people call me or think I'm a punk. It makes me feel weak. When my partner or anybody in general would call me a punk, I would always resort to physical violence. I would show them that I was not weak but stronger and better."

There is healing in the acceptance of the shame. The healthy person owns the shame and allows it to naturally dissipate. Like all similar emotional events, the shame gradually fades and is replaced by other thoughts and feelings.

In the group, when the men confessed to their shame and removed themselves enough from the subjective self to laugh about the shame, an emotional intelligence skill was achieved. A positive coping technique was learned.

One of the other group members, a pudgy younger man, followed Jake's statement about being called a punk. He said, "I am defective. People have told me that all my life." He was challenged, not by me or Don but by another inmate, who summed it up perfectly by saying, "Just because no one was there to love you does not mean you are unlovable."

This led to a discussion about balanced beliefs about oneself on the defectiveness/shame continuum. We shared with the group statements like "I am a fallible human being who makes mistakes but is still worthwhile" and "What others say or do means nothing about my self-worth."

We asked everyone to write down these rational self-statements in their notebooks. The idea was that when they thought about and believed these realistic statements, their dark moods and negative self-evaluations would shift.

Everyone began writing except Jake. He looked around, sensing he needed to get busy, to seem cooperative, and yet he clearly could not think of an affirmation for himself. He made a broad movement and began to write. The question was whether he was pretending to acknowledge the condition of shame and understanding that shame can be owned and dissipated in a healthy way. Up to that moment, Jake was reluctant to admit to being a fallible human being, one who made mistakes out of fear of acknowledging personal weakness.

In evaluating Jake and his progress in treatment, I believed Jake to be a narcissist who was generally violent and manipulated others to get what he wanted. These were all personality characteristics that suggested treatment failure. I wanted very much for Jake to change. But how realistic was that, especially after a four-month program, meeting once a week?

I imagined Jake telling someone in his unit after group, "Yeah, I just totally played Ms. Nauth. She's a sucker. She'll believe anything I say."

Yet I gave Jake a successful completion for the class. The treatment was there to teach Jake the skills to use if he wanted to change. Jake had identified some thoughts that would put him at risk for being abusive, and he wrote new beliefs that were prosocial and rational. He showed awareness of the model for changing his behavior, so I passed him. I was obliged to do so.

The last question the group members answered in their final project, the relapse prevention plan was the following:

"Indicate on a following scale of 0 to 10 the likelihood of you committing a domestic violence related offense in the future (0 is not likely at all; 10 is extremely likely)."

This question had a hidden component. If the offender picked 0, he was not being realistic and had not accepted the difficulty of change.

In a relapse prevention treatment model, once the behavior of violence becomes habitual, the individual may never feel relief from continual urges for aggression. In treatment, the individual develops a plan to cope with the urges. He must always be vigilant in order to maintain change.

In treatment, the offender needed to learn that it was likely he would slip, but each slip was a potential learning experience. It gave the offender the chance to analyze the trigger, reevaluate the action plan, and commit once again to change. Jake had written a relapse prevention plan but would probably forget it as soon as he returned to the community. I always recommend a support group in the community, but resources are such that support groups are not available. The offender is left to his own resources, and without reminders and support, the new behaviors fade out. The old behaviors return, and treatment fails.

I doubted Jake would succeed in changing his domestic violence. I don't believe that Jake had the capacity to change. He never accepted himself as the problem. If the offender is not ready, treatment can never be effective. Just because an offender completed a program, he can still be at high risk for reoffending.

In the end, I was able to prevent Jake was returning to society sooner rather than later. I recommended continued treatment in the institution rather than in the community. He would be forced to stay at FLCI until his mandatory release date.

Chapter 6

Steve and the Forty-Seven Foster Homes

My most lasting memory of Steve is of a tall, skinny, blond inmate of twenty-nine, kicking and screaming at me even as he was being restrained by three security guards. Steve had already kicked a security van door so violently that he had broken it. Steve was forcibly dragged to Fox Lake Prison's most restricted area in the segregation building. This was only two weeks after he had arrived at FLCI with a short sentence of little over a year.

That moment stands out in my memory because as Steve was struggling and yelling insults at the world, his face filled with rage. He saw me coming down the hall and screamed at me, "Cunt!"

As the men struggled with him, Steve also shouted in my direction, "Get the fuck out of my face!" This was followed by "I've got nothing to say to you!"

I was near the end of my career working with prison inmates, and this was the first time I had been called that insult, at least the first time to my face. Inmates usually do not insult staff members in front of another staff person. Disrespect is a 303.12 violation punished by five days in segregation.

The C-word seemed so harsh, even for prison. When inmates previously called me names, and they certainly did, I usually heard myself referred to as *bitch*. A bitch to them was any woman who acted in a way that they did not like. Sometimes, I had to make decisions that the inmates did not like. Ergo, I was a bitch. The opinions

I had were professional, not about my ego. Therefore, I had little reaction to the insult.

However, the word *cunt* seemed unnecessarily provocative. It was also unexpected from Steve, a young boy-man from rural Wisconsin, with wide-open eyes, scrawny, strong, with a few pimples still visible on his face. I didn't expect such hostility from him.

I didn't deserve the disrespect either. I had already met Steve a week earlier. His attitude had been hostile from the moment he walked into my office as a new intake. At our initial meeting, I introduced myself, explained our psychology department procedures, and provided a quick mental status exam.

Steve didn't care to listen to anything I had to say. He told me angrily and directly, "I have no mental health needs. You psychologists don't care about me. I've been in forty-seven foster homes, so I know. And I don't ever want to see you again."

I responded to his insulting attitude with a smile and gave my standard message, saying, "I only need to check in with you every three months if you follow the prison rules and do not get into trouble with security. At that time, I'll call you to my office. You'll need to come, stick your head in my office door, and answer a few questions. In the meantime, if you have anything you want to discuss—depression or problems with your cellmate—please write an inmate request to let me know."

Not too surprisingly, Steve didn't ask for my help. He quickly became so disruptive and violent with both staff and inmates that he no longer could function in the prison population. He was sent to segregation.

Steve's rebelliousness earned him a stark cell with a hard, thin vinyl mattress, a toilet, and sink. Two of the walls were thick, protective glass, and the cell was in a high-traffic part of the security building. Steve, forced to wear a tear-resistant smock and nothing else, was exposed to many officers regularly walking by.

A face-to-face, nonconfidential interview by the psychologist was required within sixteen hours of an inmate being given observation status. There was a psychologist on call who came into the institution to complete this interview on the weekend, holidays, and after hours.

The interview's purpose was to document that this stripping of an inmate's dignity was justified, due to clear and immediate risk of harm to himself or others. I had witnessed Steve's violent behavior and decided that if past behavior predicted future behavior, Steve needed to be given observation status.

Another purpose of the inmate interview during observation was for the psychologist to decide if any extra property items would be allowed, such as a pillow or a blanket. A blanket is usually authorized to be given by the security officers as soon as the inmate has quieted down.

Steve wanted a pillow. As I talked to him through the steel door vents, Steve's attitude turned pleasant and less contentious. Then I told him that I would not allow a pillow.

Steve used every strategy he could to get me to change my mind. He whined and pleaded and told me I was being unfair. I was following the standard procedure to allow extra property slowly in response to positive behavior.

Steve provided logic for his request. "I can't hurt myself with a pillow," he argued. He was basically correct. Segregation pillows are hard lumps of unyielding stuffing covered with a coarse, untearable type cloth.

But Steve was obviously manipulative. Every time I said "no pillow," he changed his strategy. An argument using logic came from Steve after the whining and complaining did not work. Then he tried sweet-talking me, being complimentary, and saying he understood what I went through in my job. But he was surprised when this strategy did not get him what he wanted.

When Steve finally accepted that there would be no pillow at this moment, his behavior disintegrated.

Steve went off and began pacing around the cell, muttering and swearing, yelling and spitting, throwing himself on the thin, hard mattress, and then getting up in order to gesture wildly at me, karate-kicking, and pretending to punch me, yelling details of how he would hurt me if there was no protective barrier between us.

I knew the unbreakable glass wall was between us, assuring my physical safety. Steve was not a physical threat to me. Yet I still flinched, an automatic response to his threatening behavior.

Steve's wild and out-of-control behavior continued for the next few days. Despite the intensive monitoring, Steve made two cuts on a wrist and was found bleeding in the shower. He took a twenty-minute ambulance ride from FLCI to the hospital at Waupun, population twelve thousand. At the hospital, Steve demanded pain killers and was given a small amount.

After he returned from the hospital, Steve was again placed in observation. Over the next week, he gradually started to exhibit more stable behavior. Steve became cooperative with clinical staff, denied any plans or urges to harm himself, and gradually earned back property. He was provided a regular orange jumpsuit, a blanket, and meal trays instead of sandwiches in a brown paper bag, handed through a steel trap opened with an officer's key. He stayed in the observation cell as a precaution as he waited for a conduct hearing to sentence him on his disruptive behavior and property damage.

Policy dictated that I or one of the institution clinicians see Steve every weekday and check on his mental status. This is accomplished at the inmate's steel cell door in the hallway with no privacy. After four days of my checking in with him at his door, Steve began to trust me and asked for confidential interviews, held in the segregation visiting booths.

Steve was escorted by two officers to the inmate's side of the visiting booth. I had been buzzed through a security door into the visitor's side. We were separated by a heavy glass window between us and communicated through a vent.

It was difficult to interview and/or counsel inmates in the segregation building. Not only was the setting was not pleasant but in addition, the building was damp and had a faint, bad smell. The visiting booth was small, and I had to stack the two plastic chairs on top of each other so I could see my client's eyes through the vent.

I saw Steve every few days in this so-called confidential setting but saw him at his cell door daily. He showed increasing depression, mostly, as he claimed, because he had not received any mail from his girlfriend, Angie. Angie was an older woman who he was living with before his arrest and whom he wanted to marry.

Steve could only think or talk about Angie at that point. He only remembered her good qualities, worried that he did not deserve her, and believed that if Angie stopped loving him, his life had no meaning. He told me he could not survive without her.

Steve felt sure that Angie would never communicate with him again. He was unable to contact her via his once-a-week phone calls in segregation. So he assumed the worst, jumped to the conclusion that she no longer loved him, and spent all of his moments thinking and obsessing about Angie.

Steve's anxiety about his relationship kept me from trying to discuss more immediate and pressing concerns with him, like the reasons he was in prison and what he was going to do when he was released. All I could do was listen and be supportive. Finally, after two weeks of waiting, Steve received a letter from Angie assuring him of her love.

Once Steve was in communication with Angie, much of his obsessive concern about her lessened. However, he still wanted to talk about his relationship.

"I worry she'll leave me because sometimes, I'm mean to her." Steve looked like a little boy, ashamed of himself.

"What does being mean look like?" I asked.

Steve looked sheepish. He didn't want to tell me about his shameful past behavior. But after our initial negative interactions, Steve had quickly formed a therapeutic bond with me. He knew he needed to trust me if he wanted help with his relationship.

"I called her names and put her down."

"Any physical violence?" I asked.

"Mostly hitting and shoving," he answered.

Substance abuse and domestic violence reflected the same underlying problem. Steve's difficulties originated in the significant attachment trauma secondary to forty-seven foster homes and treatment centers.

Attachment theory, founded by John Bowlby in the 1950s, proposed that the motivation to form emotional attachments with other people represents survival for humans. Bowlby considered attachment to be a biologically-based behavioral system, an instinctive response of the infant to form a stable relationship with the mother or other attachment figure.

From repeated, consistent, predictable, and nurturing caretaking experiences, the emotionally healthy infant sees his attachment figure as available. This forms a secure base in which the child can return to in threatening and stressful situations. This sense of security is imperative for the infant in developing mental and emotional health.

Support for the importance of attachment is found in the field of neuropsychology, in experiments studying mother-infant interactions and in the research on monkeys done by a man named Harry Harlow,

John Bowlby based his concept of attachment as a primate need on the work of psychologist Harlow, done at the University of Wisconsin-Madison, also conducted in the 1950s. Harlow's experiments consisted of separating baby monkeys from their mothers and studying how the infants responded.

Harlow's work was done with the Indian rhesus monkeys who showed a wide range of emotions and were able to solve puzzles similarly to human children, from the ages of two to five.

Deborah Blum tells the story of the monkey experiments in her book *Love at Goon Park*. Harry Harlow isolated infant monkeys from their mothers within six to twelve hours after birth. In one experiment, the babies were placed in a room with two surrogate mothers. The first was a cloth mother with a smiling face on a round head, with a tan terrycloth body.

The baby monkeys chose the cloth-comforting surrogate mother over a metallic surrogate, even when the metallic mother provided milk. The little monkeys rushed to the cloth mother, clutched her, and buried their faces into the warm, fluffy body. The first few times the monkeys were in the room, they never once let the cloth mother go, just held tight, and barely looked up. Eventually, the babies looked around the room, pushed a puzzle piece, chewed on a toy, but still returned to the mother as a secure, emotional base.

With only the metallic wire mother or with no surrogate mother available, the babies screeched, rocked back and forth, and sucked their hands. Without a warm, comforting surrogate mother, the baby monkeys did not explore, didn't play, and showed other signs of depression, a few refusing to eat or drink.

If adult monkeys, raised without their mothers, were placed back into a normal monkey population, they were not able to adapt to the social group. Some of these adult monkeys either stayed crouched in the corner, were bullied by the other monkeys, or attacked their peers if they tried to get too close.

Isolated monkeys proved incapable of having normal sexual relations. Artificially inseminated, one mother monkey who had been isolated held her infant's face to the floor and chewed off its feet and fingers. Another took her baby's head into her mouth and crushed it.

Although extremely troubling and now considered unethical, Dr. Harlow's experiments demonstrated the significant emotional needs of a primate infant for nurturing and comfort.

Bowlby showed that the attachment response is a biologically based behavioral system. Since then, neuroscientists have found that nurturing, caretaking, and human contact stimulates several important neurotransmitters, chemical messengers in the brain. These particular transmitters are linked with pleasure and were first studied in relation to drug addiction.

The first chemical involved is dopamine, which is connected to a sense of wanting and desire. A group of relevant chemicals is a small set of protein neurotransmitters called endorphins or enkephalins, which are endogenous opioids, also commonly called the brain's own private heroin.

When a mother nurtures a baby or when anyone acts in a nurturing way toward a child, another protein is also released in the child called oxytocin (not to be confused with the painkiller OxyContin).

Oxytocin is present when there is a nurturing connection between individuals. Oxytocin's chemistry also seems to be an essential byproduct of empathy and committed love. The joy of sex is about opioids and dopamine. But passion for your one true partner is connected to oxytocin.

In experiments with rat pups, repeated separation from the mother decreased dopamine levels and increased behavioral reactivity to stress. As adults, those rats showed decreased exploratory and social behavior and increased sensitivity to cocaine.

The neurochemicals triggered by nurturing are part of the brain's reward system, which lowers stress levels, decreases physical pain, and increases feelings of well-being.

Scientists have suggested that the biochemical processes generated by relationships are the same as those impacted by cocaine and heroin. The experience of cravings, dependency, and withdrawal are similar in both romance and addiction.

If a child receives inadequate or abusive caretaking, the developing child does whatever it takes to maintain the primary attachment relationship. He or she develops stable maladaptive behavior and response strategies to adapt to a less than optimal caregiving environment.

In a famous study of infant-maternal interaction called the *Strange Experiment,* Mary Ainsworth, an American psychologist in the '60s and '70s, set up a fascinating research paradigm in which one-year-old babies were observed with their mothers in a pleasant, toy-filled room.

The experiment involved the child's response to increasing levels of threat: a stranger entered the room, and after a few minutes, the mother left. The next phase was a reunion scene, which ended the twenty-minute experiment.

The attachment hypothesis was that entrance of the stranger would trigger the predictable, biologically based separation distress, and prompt the child to seek proximity to his or her mother. The increase in attachment behavior was accompanied by an equal decrease of the child's exploratory (play) behavior.

A secure child in the Strange Experiment played happily with the toys, looking at his/her mother a few times for reassurance. When the stranger entered, the child's level of arousal increased, and as attachment theory predicts, the child craved proximity to the mother as a source of protection and safety.

The secure child demonstrated the expected separation distress at the mother's departure. When the mother returned, the secure child stretched out his/her arms eagerly to the mother and was quickly comforted by a hug and reassurance. The child then became once again interested in playing and exploring.

Secure children seemed to expect their mothers to be attentive, helpful, and encouraging and learned that if they became distressed, the mother would help them regain a sense of security. Secure children internalized a sense of their mother as an inner source of safety and comfort.

Three insecure attachment styles were observed during the Strange Experiment: There was an anxious/preoccupied pattern, a fearful/avoidant style, and a disorganized response.

An anxious/preoccupied attachment style found the child clinging to his/her mother, too preoccupied with the mother's whereabouts to explore freely. When separated from the mother, the anxious/preoccupied child showed extremely high levels of physiological distress compared to secure children, determined by a rapid increase in the child's heart rate.

When the mother returned, the anxious child proved difficult to comfort, continued to show high attachment arousal, and was slow to return to play.

In the avoidant attachment pattern, the child paid little attention to the mother, focusing on playing with the toys. The child seemed unconcerned when the mother left and actively snubbed her at the reunion.

Yet while appearing unfazed during separation, the avoidant child reacted physiologically, showing that actual distress was undeniable. Heart rates during the separation episodes were as high as those of visibly distressed children and cortisol levels (the body's principal stress hormone) were significantly greater than those of secure children.

Some children displayed behavior that was inexplicable, contradictory, or bizarre. During the reunion, some children froze in place, collapsed to the floor, became limp, or appeared to be in a dazed, trancelike state.

Attachment styles were found to be associated with different parenting approaches. A preoccupied style was developed when the mother's attention was inconsistent and the child never felt safe. Mothers of children found to be avoidant had actively rejected their children and withdrew when the child appeared to be sad. Disorganized attachment occurred when the child, preprogrammed to turn to a primary attachment figure when feeling threatened, found this figure to be the source of the danger.

The attachment style demonstrated at age one follows an individual throughout his or her lifespan. John Bowlby observed that attachment plays a vital role in the life of a person from cradle to grave. In the 1980s, the field of adult attachment began to evolve. Longitudinal studies showed an 80 percent continuity rate between infant and adult attachment patterns.

In Donald Dutton's research, domestic violence perpetrators were found to show higher attachment insecurity than the general population. Emotionally volatile offenders showed a preoccupied attachment style, while generally violent men exhibited avoidant attachment styles.

Avoidant styles are divided into two categories: fearful avoidant or angry and dismissive avoidant. Both styles share an unconscious fear that others are unreliable and intimacy is dangerous. The dismissive avoidant individual has made a complete transformation and decided that he/she does not need relationships. The fearful offender still craves attachment but experiences pervasive interpersonal distrust and fear of emotional intimacy.

Steve's ability to achieve attachment security was disrupted by his extremely high number of foster care placements. Initially, his out-of-home placements corresponded to his mother's hospitalizations for suicide attempts. When he was four years old, Steve's mother, who struggled with alcohol as well as mental health problems, gave up custody of Steve to the county social and human services department. She could not control Steve's aggressive and self-abusive behavior.

Steve's uncontrollable behavior led to a lengthy series of foster home placements, and at age twelve, he spent fifteen months at a juvenile treatment facility called Carmelite Home for Boys in Waukesha, Wisconsin, run by a group of nuns.

Each separation, from one home to the next, degraded Steve's ability to gain a sense of security and attachment to a primary caretaker. How could any child survive forty-seven foster home placements?

My therapy sessions with Steve improved when he was released from segregation. He visited me in my office, where I was more comfortable and able to concentrate on what Steve was telling me. I finally was able to hear Steve recall his past.

Steve shared memories of watching his mother purposely cut herself, screaming and cursing, followed by the police coming to take her to the hospital. Steve told me he remembered he was four years old at the time and when the police and the ambulance left, he was alone in the house. I imagined the horror on his face, a child realizing he was on his own and didn't know what to do.

He remembered being angry as a child and believing that he must be bad because each family sent him on and no one kept him. He said he was once going to be adopted by what seemed to be a very nice family but at the last minute, they moved away and he was again left behind.

After Steve shared these memories of abandonment, I asked, "How did these experiences shape who you are now as an adult?" To help him answer, I told Steve about attachment theory and the Strange Experiment.

The Strange Experiment showed how different children responded in different ways to childhood trauma. The attachment styles presented different behavioral strategies to cope with suboptimal parenting.

After I explained how the avoidant child acted like he didn't care about his mother, Steve interrupted me and said, "I was like the kid who just played with the toys. I gave up on my mother at an early age."

There were two possible attachment avoidant styles, and I concluded that Steve was fearful-avoidant rather than dismissive-avoidant. Steve had already shown me his strong attachment drive. He wanted intimacy and a close relationship with Angie. Yet his fear of closeness seemed to be getting in his way.

I told him this and informed him that the fearful attachment style was characterized by approach avoidance, alternating between an anxious/preoccupied strategy to attain love and an avoidant pattern of fearing love and pushing it away.

Steve nodded, seeing a connection. "I wanted to be close but then she'd feel too close. I'd feel I was suffocating, I felt trapped."

I asked, "What were you afraid of? Why was intimacy so scary?"

Steve paused and answered in a quiet voice, "I was afraid to show her who I really was. I felt myself to be inadequate and generally no good. How could I be comfortable showing myself to her? If she really got to know me, she'd reject me.

"I'd avoid her and close up. But then I would become lonely, and when the loneliness became unbearable, I'd again try to engage her. I'd seek out intimacy and my loneliness would lessen."

I felt him finally opening up and being willing to face dark truths, so I pushed gently on. "But why would you call Angie names or hit her?"

"I'd get angry because I never felt loved and safe. I'd get mad whenever I'd feel Angie pull away from me."

I was glad he was putting his behavior into a category, naming a feeling. He was gaining insight into how his defense's interfered with his goal of intimacy. Attachment theory seemed to provide a model to help explain Steve's relationship dysfunction.

But there was more to uncover in Steve's history. Steve seemed to flip from aggressive approach behavior to an anxious-preoccupied and then avoidant strategy in seemingly unpredictable ways. Steve's adult attachment style sometimes slipped into a disorganized style, a state in which the person's behavioral strategies break down. Steve's chaotic and self-abusive behavior in observation status when I first met him seemed to characterize this sense of a total lack of a coherent style for coping.

"Tell me more about your mother," I asked.

Steve looked uncomfortable. "My mother tried to kill me. Three times."

My breathing stopped for a moment. I took a pause and leaned forward to encourage him.

He continued. "I remember during the summer playing outside and, for some reason, felt frightened. I went running into the house wanting her to comfort me. She was in the kitchen and had a knife in her hand. She said I'd better not bother her and started shouting at me. I was more scared of her than anything."

"What reminds you of that memory as an adult?" I asked.

Steve told me, "When I was in observation and banging my head against the glass, I heard my mother's voice screaming obscenities at me from behind my shoulder. I felt frozen, and the only way I could make her voice go away was to bang my head."

"Your mother is supposed to be a source of safety," I reassured him as best as I could. "But instead she was the source of danger."

Steve slumped a bit. "I'm broken. What's going to help me?"

"I know it's hard."

I continually reflected on my own personal difficulties with attachment whenever I spoke to inmates on the topic. I don't believe those who counsel others should ever forget the universal human problem of being wired for love while confronting real-life experiences of rejection and abandonment regularly.

"There's an attachment style called earned security," I told Steve. "It is possible to develop a secure adult attachment style even though your early relationships screwed you up.

"The strategy for creating an earned secure adult attachment style involves reflecting on your childhood experiences and making sense of the impact the past has on your present and future."

And although the advice is trite and overused, one of the last things I said to Steve, the man who called me the worst name you can call a woman, before he was released, was "You can learn to love yourself."

CHAPTER 7

Jonathan and Beast:
Two Minds in the Same Body

I met Jonathan, a black twenty-nine-year-old inmate in November of 2006. He was a new transfer to Fox Lake Correctional and I met with him in my office for clinical monitoring. Jonathan was sent to Fox Lake prison to attend school and obtain his HSED. Jonathan was short, 5'8", with a slight but toned physique. His hair was dark; his face was also thin and very serious.

I did not meet Beast, Jonathan's violent alter ego, until August 2007. Jonathan was my first and only client exhibiting symptoms of Multiple Personality Disorder (MPD) now known as Dissociative Identity Disorder (DID).

The idea of two or more distinct identities/personalities, also known as alters, taking control of the individual's behavior is difficult to imagine. How do multiple personalities exist simultaneously while occupying one body? How could the conscious mind split into multiple identities, each with a separate set of memories, attitudes, beliefs, fears, and dreams?

Jonathan was serving his second incarceration for gang violence. Psychological reports from his first incarceration in 2005–2007 indicated Jonathan met with psychological staff a few times to discuss the death of an infant daughter ten years before. None of the psychologists or treatment staff documented any signs of mental illness. He completed treatment programs and showed no behavior problems.

Upon returning to Dodge Correctional Institution on 1/7/09, the reports note Jonathan disclosed that he had been hearing voices since the age of six. He was started on Risperidone, an antipsychotic medication to help manage the voices and stop his thoughts of hurting people. The medications were discontinued a few months later.

Records discussed a trauma history: As a six-year-old, Jonathan was anally and violently raped by an adolescent cousin who babysat him while his mother worked. The abuse was discovered when Jonathan went to the hospital with rectal bleeding and scaring. His mother was described as caring but ineffectual.

At age fourteen, Jonathan violently assaulted his cousin putting his abuser into the hospital. He joined a gang and became a leader, known for brutal and seemingly unprovoked violence. At age seventeen, he was incarcerated at EAS, the state's juvenile facility.

At our first interview, Jonathan was quiet and spoke softly. He was a bit scattered in his speech. He'd sometimes start one subject and switch to another; but overall, his thoughts seemed coherent and goal-directed. He was pleasant, and well-mannered, indicating an interest in psychology because of his behavior problems as a juvenile.

Jonathan wanted to tell me about his baby dying. "I was seventeen years old and had just been sent to EAS when she died. I couldn't handle it and went crazy. I still was in love with her mother. We are still in an on again, off again relationship. Even though I've been violent."

Jonathan thought he functioned better off psychotropic medications. "They don't help and just made me feel weird." Jonathan assured me that he was now in control of the voices and was progressing in his goals of getting his HSED.

At our next monitoring session, three months later, Jonathan continued to assert his positive functioning off medication. He still heard the voices. Describing the voices, he said, "The voices talk about the sexual abuse." Jonathan portrayed the voices as negative speaking to him in his head in the second-person narrative. Jonathan's voices said "I hate you" versus an intrusive thought of "I hate myself." The voices were critical, intimidating, and threatening.

While popular belief and media portrayal suggests that hearing voices within one's head is relatively uncommon in a general population, the incidence is actually much higher. Non psychiatric research subjects endorsed the statement "I've had the experience of hearing voices in my head." However, voices in a normal population were usually characterized as positive, providing guidance, information, encouragement, or support.

Voices of non-mentally ill individuals typically were assigned to a particular identity, a defined relationship with the voices, and experiencing the voice as "real" even if the individual objectively acknowledged the voices as unreal. Voices are often underreported because of the common fear of being diagnosed as crazy.

Negative voices either criticizing or encouraging the harming of oneself or are associated with early psychological trauma histories. Several research studies cited in Paul Frewen and Ruth Lanius's 2015 book *Healing the Traumatized Self: Consciousness, Neuroscience and Treatment* found the likelihood of hearing voices increased significantly with a higher number of types of childhood trauma, i.e., a higher number of ACES.

Conscious narrative thought is experienced in the first-person perspective; traumatized patients report voices from a second-person perspective. Instead of the person orating his own life story, another narrative voice speaks inside his head. The negatively toned voices are intrusive, unwanted, distressing, and experienced as beyond the individual's control.

The next time I saw Jonathan, a few months later on November 21, he was in segregation for fighting with another inmate. In a confidential interview held in the visiting booth, Jonathan told me he was disappointed in himself for getting into a fight and ending up in segregation.

Jonathan said, "I become a different person when I'm angry. The voices are squeezing to get out and screaming, pushing me to do things I don't want to do."

Eventually, Jonathan admitted that there was only one voice and the voice belonged to Beast. Jonathan explained that Beast was a different person from Jonathan. "Beast does all the fighting. He's strong and takes care of me."

Beast was a gang member and held a position high in the gang hierarchy. Jonathan described Beast as ruthless and cold-hearted, respected in the gang for his brutality when he felt threatened or wanted retribution.

Beast was a different person but existed inside of him. Beast was inside his head, commenting on our interaction. Head bent, Jonathan told me, "Beast is not happy. He tells me not to trust you. He says you're trying to hurt us."

When seen on November 28, Jonathan was out of segregation, and I called him up to my office for a follow-up appointment. He walked in and sat down impatiently, with an attitude of disgust, complaining, "Jonathan is weak. Jonathan is inside of me, whining and crying but I won't let him out. He's always whining about doing the right thing, but that's just weak talk and he'll get over that."

Jonathan's usual polite and agreeable self was no longer in evidence. He now was angry and hostile, spiced with contempt. "Meeting you was a waste of time," he said.

"Jonathan only needs me. You'd be useless. You'd never be able to protect him."

Beast never introduced himself as an individual separate from Jonathan. Arrogance led him to assume I knew Beast was in charge. His posture was straighter; his tone of voice was stronger and more commanding. He looked directly into my eyes. His attitude was anti-social; he bragged about hurting people when they made him angry.

Beast's initial disdain for Jonathan changed to overprotectiveness. "I tell the little dude there's no one else who can help him like me."

At the end of the session, Beast turned back into Jonathan. Now sad and deflated, this Jonathan said, "I need Beast. I don't want him to leave. He's the only one I can depend on."

The next month, Jonathan got into another fight and was placed in segregation. When pulled him out of his cell to speak to him in visiting booth, Jonathan tried to explain to me why he was in segregation.

"I was talking to another inmate in the dayroom when another inmate barged into the conversation and became loud and aggressive." He said, "I don't remember anything after that until I was talking to the security captain about the fight. Beast was in my head telling me about the fight and laughing.

"I need Beast. He came when I wanted him. That's the way it's supposed to work."

In later sessions, Jonathan said, "Beast comes even when I don't call on him. There's no way I can control him."

This time in segregation, Jonathan decided that he wanted to try medications again. He said, "The meds would stop me from getting angry. I'd get angry, but Beast couldn't react."

I referred Jonathan to the psychiatrist. On December 3, he was put on the list to see Dr. S from 2:30 to 3:00. The psychiatrist's time is valuable and he needed to see eight segregation inmates about their medications. Security arranges three segregation inmates to be in the three separate tiny closets, called the visiting booths, at all times. On the other side of the wall, Dr. S went from one inmate to another to discuss medication.

Jonathan was in the middle booth. He could see Dr. S talking to the inmate on his right and he knew he would be next. But Dr. S skipped his booth to meet with the inmate on Jonathan's left. Jonathan got angry and asked to be taken back to his cell. He refused to wait for the psychiatrist. The consequence for his refusal was that he was placed back on the waiting list and it would be a few weeks before he could be scheduled again.

I was not happy with Jonathan. We had decided that medication might be helpful to him, and now he had sabotaged the plan. When I interviewed him the next day, Jonathan did not remember getting angry and walking out of the visiting booth.

He remembered, "It was my turn and the psychiatrist skipped me and went to the next inmate. I thought he disrespected me. I blacked out." Then he reflected a moment and said, "Beast must have walked out. He doesn't want me to take medication."

I was faced with a diagnostic dilemma. Jonathan was presenting with two personalities—Jonathan, a quiet, thoughtful man with prosocial goals; and Beast, a strong fighter who protected the weaker Jonathan. Did Jonathan meet the criteria for the diagnosis of multiple personality disorder?

In the DSM-IV *Diagnostic Statistical Manual*, the bible of psychological mental disorders, a multiple personality disorder (MPD), now known as *dissociative identity disorder* (DID) is defined as two or more very distinct and enduring personality states, each with its own enduring pattern of perceiving, relating to, and thinking about the environment and self. At least two of the identities or personality states recurrently take control of the person's behavior.

DID is the most complex and severe of the dissociative disorders and the most controversial. Advocates of MPD believe that in response to severe trauma, the child's identity is fragmented into two or more distinct personality states. Only one personality interacts with the external environment at one time.

The different personalities are called *alters*. Transitions between each alter is known as *switching*. Each alter has his or her own autobiographical memories, thoughts, feelings, and attitudes. Persons with DID do not believe they have several personalities but several different and distinct people.

DID was called multiple personality disorder until 1994, when the name changed to reflect a better understanding of the process of dissociation, a splintering of identity rather than the growth of separate identities. The terms MPD and DID can be used interchangeably.

Skeptics are positive that MPD is a make-believe, fake diagnosis. Some assert that MPD was originally created through hypnosis. After watching popular movies and books like *Sybil a*nd *Three Faces of Eve,* the therapist, a true believer, suggests, shapes, and molds the patient's behavior into acting like he has MPD. The client finds MPD a theory that helps describe, explains, and express their conflicting feeling and thoughts.

In the legal system and corrections, MPD is easily dismissed as malingering. The offender is deliberately play-acting, trying to use insanity to avoid punishment for their crime. Defendants also claim that another alter committed the offense and therefore cannot be held responsible.

All these extra issues and controversies around a MPD diagnosis triggered anxiety for me. The reason for my uneasiness lay in an article I read in 1984 in the *Isthmus*—a free, weekly, and liberally biased newspaper based in Madison, Wisconsin. The article told of an inmate from Waupun Correctional Institution claimed he had multiple personality disorders and was mentally ill. He was suing the state to transfer him from the Department of Corrections to the state Department of Health and Human Services. The state did not consider the diagnosis true, valid, or reliable.

The *Isthmus* slanted the story with themes of "Goliath versus David," the state against the disenfranchised inmate and good versus evil. I remember reading the article with a sense of gratitude. I was glad that I was not the psychologist in that contentious environment.

Now, in 2009, while in session with Jonathan, I started thinking and worrying. If I really believed Jonathan to be a multiple, I might be forced to argue my diagnosis in court, defending my opinion against many, many people who wanted to prove me wrong. Also, Jonathan was claiming that Beast perpetrated the violence and could be projecting the responsibility for the violence.

I didn't know what to think. I had some suspicions that Jonathan might be faking. Beast didn't seem like a real person but a cartoon character without true dimension or depth. Jonathan's movements as Beast seemed wooden rather than spontaneous. Jonathan seemed to be uneasy whenever he talked about Beast.

Truthfully, from my own limited experience with MPD, I expected a more dramatic change from one personality to the other. When I observed Jonathan switch to Beast and back again, the changes were subtle. I didn't observe different speech patterns, voice tones, mannerisms, or even a sense of different ages. When Beast said he was in control of the body, I saw Jonathan become more arrogant, angry, and aggressive, but he was still Jonathan. I saw two different sides of a personality, not two different personalities.

Evidence for Jonathan being a genuine multiple was limited but compelling. Jonathan linked the first appearance of Beast at age six while experiencing a violent rape by his cousin. MPD and DID are linked with extreme, sadistic, and bizarre abuse.

I concluded that Jonathan's adolescent cousin, raging with angry hormones, forced to babysit this stupid kid, brutally took his aggression out on this six-year-child. Apparently, the cousin was sufficiently violent to tear Jonathan's rectum to cause an emergency room visit. This certainly fits the definition of severe trauma. The cousin easily also could have been sadistic, i.e., the abuser gets pleasure from the violence.

I could only guess whether the cousin's beating were unexpected or ritualized, either scenario equally terrifying to a six-year-old Jonathan.

During the abuse, as his cousin is repeatedly punching and kicking him, Jonathan experienced indescribable terror. He had no way of protecting himself against this bully, and his mother wasn't coming to help him. He believed he was going to die.

In the literature on dissociative identity disorder, different kinds of voices or patterns are described. A *protective* or *rescuer* alter personality is created to save the original personality from intolerable condition. Jonathan imagined Beast intervening by fighting or running away.

Neuropsychologists believe that modes of representing the internal world changes as the child grows. From age two to the ages of six or seven, the child thinks concretely. He uses a reasoning of *psychic-equivalence* in which the child equates his mental state with reality. In *pretend mode of thinking*, internal cognition separates from reality in a dissociative process.

Jonathan's reasoning includes both psychic equivalence and the pretend mode. Thoughts are experienced as reality, but in the next moment, his thoughts become disconnected from the real world. In order to help him cope with the violent rape, Jonathan imagines a protector with superhuman strength and bravery. In his mind, he uses psychic equivalence and believes that his hero is real. His hero lives in a comic book world, separate from reality and experienced in a dissociative state.

Compared to Beast, Jonathan feels weak and shamed by the abuse. His protector adds a *persecutor personality* and starts to blame Jonathan for the abuse, taunting him and telling Jonathan he needs to die or pay for succumbing to the abuser. The persecutor tells Jonathan he is weak, useless, and worthless.

Jonathan acts like Beast in relationship to his abusive cousin. Beast stands up against the abusive cousin. In the development of a dissociative identity disorder, Jonathan becomes Beast in a trancelike state, and the child uses a trancelike state in order to remove his mental awareness of the unbearable situation. Ordinary consciousness (state of mind A: Jonathan) is periodically interrupted by (state of mind B: Beast) with each repeated stressor. As with self-hypnotic amnesia, when Jonathan returns to state of mind A, he does not remember what Beast did in state of mind B.

With repeated alternation, state of mind B, Beast, becomes more and more elaborated with a sense of continuity giving the state of mind a set of emotionally related memories and a history. Gradually, Beast organizes as an identity with characteristic emotions, a sense of self, and a distinct way of relating to the abuser.

An important step in the development of a DID is giving the altered state of mind and identity a different name. Assigning a name to the different state of mind consolidates the process, giving some order to the fragmentation. Once given a name, the dissociative defense can be employed more automatically.

Jonathan told me that Beast gained his name when Jonathan was age fourteen and assaulted his cousin severely enough to put him into the hospital.

Additional evidence of a major break from reality came from Jonathan describing coping with the death of his infant daughter. He was age seventeen, an age associated with psychosis—separation from reality. He told me that his behavior was out of control, and he spent time in segregation and observation placement, solitary confinement exacerbated his problems with his auditory hallucinations.

"The voices got stronger and I went crazy," Jonathan said.

If Jonathan had exhibited two personalities as an adult, being in a gang allowed a logical nexus between Jonathan and Beast. He told me, "Beast was my street name." Apparently, he would function well as Beast in the street violence. He could function well as Jonathan when he rejected a violent philosophy and engaged in the societal game of trying to be good.

I did not really need to make an official diagnosis while working with Jonathan. The diagnostic manual allowed for a Rule/out (R/O) mind-set. The diagnosis R/O indicated that I thought Jonathan was most likely a genuine multiple, but I allowed for future evidence against a diagnosis of MPD. My decision was deferred.

Regardless of my profession interpretation, during our sessions, I related to Jonathan and Beast as separate identities. Once, I negotiated with Beast to allow Jonathan to take psychotropic medications. Never sure that Jonathan was not putting on an act, I felt uncomfortable addressing him directly.

Luckily, my interaction time with Beast was limited. And I treated Jonathan similar to the way I worked with antisocial offenders. But instead of relating to two opposite extremes of one personality, I was working with two separate but still opposing types of personality.

Most violent offenders have some sense of an inner metaphorical moral divide between their good side and their bad side. Often, I refer the inmates to a cartoon of a man, behind a tree, looking at some apples hanging in the apple orchard next door. The apples are big and ripe and very tempting.

In the cartoon, a devil is drawn hovering over the man's left shoulder saying, "Steal them. You deserve those apples. You deserve to feel good, no matter who it hurts." An angel is drawn over the man's right side telling him, "no, no, and no."

The cartoon depicts a universal theme in humankind: Man's decision to choose between good and evil. In violent offenders, the choice is very relevant. Will I use aggression (violate another's rights) to get what I want? Or violate my own rights, needs, desires to give someone else what they want?

To a violent offender, the decision is binary. One wins and the other loses. Black and white. All-or-nothing thinking—two opposing points of view with no middle road. Jonathan could only be all bad or all good.

Jonathan wanted Beast to stop interfering in his life. He knew that if Beast kept up his violence, he would keep coming back to prison and eventually prison would become his life. He said, "I can't mess up again." He knew Beast would continue to thwart any progress until Jonathan controlled him.

But as usual, change was difficult.

On 12/4, while still in segregation for the fight, Jonathan defended Beast for protecting him. He sat across from me in the segregation visiting booth. I could see only the top of his head. His head was down and he said, "Beast reacted aggressively when he was supposed to. Someone was trying to hurt me."

I asked Jonathan to identify times when Beast was not so helpful. "That's easy," he said. Currently in his life, Beast was looming as a large obstacle:

"My ex-wife and son want to come visit me in prison, but I'm not sure. She wants to get back with me. I'm afraid to go home to her. Beast was violent with her, and I'm afraid he might hurt my son."

Usually, the violent offender knows that he has both good and evil within his own personality, or soul. I don't have to convince them that the two opposing sides are part of his personality. For Jonathan, the good and evil were on different planets. And Jonathan rejected all of his own anger and projected it onto Beast.

Jonathan asserted, "I'm not angry. Anger hurts people. I'm a good guy."

Jonathan was spouting a common axiom in the offender population. It dismisses the possibility that people are either always good or always bad. He is using dichotomous, black-or-white reasoning. The logical counter is that people can be good and sometimes act badly.

Anger levels also exist on a continuum. I grabbed a piece of paper and drew a scale from one to ten. I pointed to the lower numbers on the left side of the scale and said, "If you don't get something you want or someone is standing as an obstacle to a goal, you are going to be angry. This anger can be healthy. The anger will motivate you to problem-solve and change the situation if you can. But it's important to keep the level of anger low, at a 3 or 4 level.

"But what happens if you are at an 8, 9, or 10 level of anger?" I pointed to the upper numbers on the scale. I answered the question. "You make poor decisions about your behavior. You become aggressive and hurt people."

I said to Jonathan, "At a low level of anger, you won't hurt anyone."

Jonathan seemed wary and skeptical. He had already denied experiencing any anger because "anger is bad." His anger was unacceptable to him, and he coped by projecting it onto Beast.

I encouraged him to think about the possibility that Beast represented his own anger. "Try it on like you'd try on a pair of pants you wanted to buy. See if it fits, see if it makes sense."

Jonathan left the January session unconvinced that anger could be experienced and managed without anyone getting hurt. I set our next meeting in a month. Jonathan's motivation for treatment vacillated. Though I would have liked to spend more time with Jonathan, he was not asking to do the work of therapy. I didn't really have time, and honestly, I had no training with this diagnosis; psychologists are supposed to defer from working with issues beyond their expertise. Since I was the only clinician available, I provided the anger management skill training and hoped that my efforts would pay off. I was not optimistic.

Amazingly, at our February session, Jonathan announced that he and Beast had come "to an understanding. I'll talk the problem through, and if that doesn't work, Beast can jump in later." That day, Jonathan presented with a very rational view of anger.

Jonathan told me, "Being angry is not the problem, it's what you do when you are angry." He described ways he could be assertive in conflict situations rather than aggressive. He shared an angering situation with his son's mother and indicated he had responded rationally.

Listening to Jonathan, I was surprised and amazed. Jonathan was showing a complete change in philosophy, almost impossible within one month and after only one session of anger management. Jonathan was also reading an autobiography by the Chicago Bulls' basketball coach, who discussed his own struggles with a temper. It still seemed amazingly quick.

When meeting the next month, Jonathan said, "I'm doing fine." He admitted, "I still have those days I want to slap the dude. Beast tells me to 'go ahead and slap the bitch.' I stay in control and know violence will lead to no good."

Jonathan continued, "I tell Beast that even if the situation looks bad, it's probably not." The positive self-talk seemed to calm both of them. Jonathan appeared to be thinking in a more rational mode. Still, his next statement pulled him back.

"I'm going to cut everyone out of my life. I'm going to live like a hermit. I prefer to be alone."

Jonathan claimed, "Sooner or later, everyone is going to hurt you."

Jonathan agreed to consider the possibility of protecting himself while still engaging with others. He had developed a working relationship with Beast and overall appeared more balanced and confident.

I didn't see Jonathan for two more months. During our next session, Jonathan said, "I'm able to control Beast now and tell him to relax when he gets angry." Still, Jonathan was worried.

"Beast hates the box [segregation]. He knows he has to listen to me as long as we're still in prison. But what happens when I get out and negative consequences are not so clear or immediate? Beast will probably retake control when we're back in the community. I know I won't be able to stay away from the gang and violence. I know I'll return to prison with a life sentence."

Later in the session, Jonathan discussed his difficulty in deciding to go back to Racine or transfer out of state to live with his mother in Arizona. Getting away from Wisconsin, Jonathan said, "I think I can stay away from the street life, get a job, and live a better life." His mother was now sober and living responsibly.

I met with Jonathan five more times over the next seven months. In four of those sessions, he used prosocial reasoning to discuss decisions where to live, how he wanted to be a father to his son, and what he wanted from his relationship with his ex. He was future-oriented.

He was thoughtful and reflective. He was responsive to the input I offered about a new option or a new perspective.

One day, Jonathan reverted to his antisocial philosophy. His mother had failed to complete the paperwork so that Jonathan could live with her in Arizona. He believed her lack of action meant that she no longer wanted him to live with her. He termed her failure to support him as abandonment but then denied feeling hurt.

He said, "I don't feel bad, I just accept it." His gaze traveled to somewhere in the distance, and he grew rigid. He became dismissive of his mother and proclaimed, "The only one I can trust is me," "I'll do anything to survive," and "I need Beast now." On that date, he told me politely that he no longer wanted to explore his feelings with me.

"What good is feeling hurt going to get me? Feelings are weak." Jonathan expressed a Beast-type worldview where others are cruel and unforgiving and only the strong survive.

Overall, in those last few sessions, Jonathan was positive and future-oriented. He referred to Beast only intermittently and usually to the effect of "I don't need Beast" and "I control Beast." Beast no longer seemed an issue in Jonathan's life.

As I write this chapter, I now believe in the diagnosis of dissociative identity disorder caused by childhood trauma. I also wonder if other inmates I've worked with in the past, offenders like Stephen (chapter 4) may also have been DID. In his state of dissociation and amnesia, another personality may have been operating, with his own consciousness, separate and unknown by Stephen.

Central to DID is the presence of two or more distinct identities or personality states that recurrently take control of behavior. Each personality has his own relatively enduring pattern of perceiving, relating to, and thinking about self and others. In DID, the parts are completely separated so that in each self-state, the patient experiences radical differences in his behavior, feelings, and sense of identity. Each self-state has a different personality.

Violent men seem to experience a similar splitting into an aggressive versus a non-aggressive state of mind. In DID, the two parts of self emerge as separate identities. For many violent men, the two parts are less well-defined, existing as opposing philosophies or values. The different parts do not represent a different person but a different and opposing part of their personality.

Jeff Young defines this distinct and separate state of mind as a schema mode. Schemas and coping patterns tend to group together into parts of the self. Certain clusters of schema and/or coping responses are triggered together, which collate into characteristic groupings. For example, Young identifies a *vulnerable child mode*, the suffering inner child who experiences the emotional pain defining the schema—"I am helpless, I am unlovable." The *angry child mode* counterattacks the schema by becoming aggressive when his basic emotional needs are not met.

The schema mode of the violent offender could be characterized as a set of antisocial attitudes, values, and beliefs that lead an individual to choose aggression. The hypothetical schema mode would be dominated by the mistrust/abuse schema, counterattacking a powerless schema by power and control and transforming a schema of emotional deprivation into entitlement.

Usually in my work with violent offenders, I help the inmate identify arguments for the prosocial self and against the antisocial mind-set. This is the role I took with Jonathan. I allied myself with Jonathan to fight against his aggressive state of mind. Jonathan and most offenders eventually appreciate that being prosocial was more logical, rational, and within his best interests.

Violence itself can be seen as reflecting a dissociative process. Intense anger arousal may trigger the alternative state of consciousness. Emotional management skills would prevent the dissociation process from occurring. Rather, Jonathan was taught how to lower his level of anger and avoid the emergence of the Beast state of mind. Jonathan was also encouraged to integrate his anger into his Jonathan self rather than deny it.

If Jonathan and Beast were two different identities, with Beast perpetrating the violence, who is responsible? Should the individual be held responsible for actions in the dissociated state?

Yes. Taking responsibility is at the core of treatment. It is a major step between continuity and integration of experience. While the dissociative process acts automatically and unconsciously, the patient can learn control over the switching process, and control over destructive behavior in the altered states of mind. It is not easy.

In Jonathan's case, both Beast and Jonathan took responsibility for the violence. Jonathan blamed himself for allowing Beast to take over. Jonathan never complained that he was being blamed for something; someone else did.

As quoted in *Coping with Trauma: A Guide to Self-Understanding* by Jon G. Allen, "We need to honor the most precious of all human possessions: basic autonomy, with its fundamental correlate, personal responsibility."

CHAPTER 8

Maria, the Domestic Violence Victim

I met Maria when I was a volunteer facilitator of a women's support group at the local women's shelter in Beaver Dam. People Against a Violent Environment, Inc. (PAVE) is a nonprofit organization providing free and confidential support for those affect by domestic violence. PAVE offered our small community crisis counseling, temporary housing for female and child victims of abuse (a twenty-two-bed shelter), and support in learning a violence-free lifestyle. I met Maria while facilitating the women's support group.

At age thirty, Maria had left her abuser for the second time and was living at the shelter, again with her children, Luke, age eight, and Callie, age six. Right away, Maria stood out from the other group members. She was verbal, bright, and passionate.

I found Maria beautiful with warm, soft brown skin and high cheekbones. Her figure was petite and she wore her obviously thrift store clothes with a fun and individual style. She wore just enough make-up to highlight large beautiful eyes with long, dark lashes.

Maria's most striking quality was intense and animated storytelling. Even during that first group session, Maria drew the attention of the other group members, monopolizing the time, although I don't think anyone objected. Maria dramatized her stories, acted out intense emotional highs and lows, and made everyone laugh with comical facial expressions and mimicry.

Yet Maria was always in crisis; her life was chaotic and her problems were immediate and urgent. For Maria, life was a struggle, with obstacles, setbacks, and hurt feelings. She saw herself as a fighter, alone with two children and no one to support her. She described feeling stuck. "I want to kill myself but I can't die. No one would take care of my children."

She didn't talk a lot about her childhood, but her stories about her more recent struggles suggested a dysfunctional family with a physically abusive mother. Maria told us about a period of homelessness when she finally asked her mother if she and the children could live in her mother's home. She knew at the time she could not depend on her mother: "My mother was never helpful before in my life, but I was desperate.

"We lived with her just for two days. I left real quick after I came into the living room from the kitchen and saw my mother with her hands around Luke's neck, choking him."

Maria's stories, even those involving serious abuse and violence, usually ended with a comic twist. Maria would make a cute gesture that somehow made fun of her predicament. She exaggerated a sense of irony and absurdity in her never-ending battle against a cruel world.

One story Maria told the group involved Maria's predicament at the end of her first stay at PAVE. The average stay was six to eight weeks, and with staff support, women were expected to find their own residence. Maria had already been in the shelter for four months. Maria had applied for social security disability but still hadn't heard whether she would qualify. She couldn't find anyone to rent to her because she didn't have a steady income and had no money for a security deposit.

"I finally went to a rundown house outside the city. It wasn't much, but there was a small backyard and I imagined my kids playing there.

"The landlord seemed nice at first. He wanted to help me and told me I could rent the house cheap. I was thinking finally something good was happening. But then he asked me for sex."

The other women in the group gasped at how evil the landlord was. I felt indignation myself against him for trying to take advantage of Maria's vulnerability. I recalled how I felt when my professor propositioned me in an effort to empathize. I was set to help Maria as a victim.

But Maria seemed unfazed. "Not the first time that happened," Maria noted without self-pity. She expected such behavior from men. She said she had been sexually assaulted before the age of nine. It was no big deal. Being a sexual object and a victim was a familiar role.

Maria was stuck in a life trap. In her life as an adult, she was recreating the victimization she experienced in her childhood. Being taken advantage of sexually seemed familiar to Maria. If I asked, I bet she would admit that being manipulated and used for sex was an ongoing activity with different men and different times.

The landlord had sensed a sexual vulnerability in Maria. I could see it too. In her animation and dramatic movements, there was a faint but unmistakable sensuality. Like Marilyn Monroe, Maria's beauty included a seductive quality. Unconsciously, she wanted to attract men. A learned behavior, her sexuality was part of her. It was only through sexuality that she had survived as a child.

And most importantly, Maria expected men to proposition her sexually. She expected others to abuse her. Maria experienced herself to be a highly desirable sexual object but remained innocently and consciously unaware. This was a schema for Maria. A perception of herself, how others saw her, and how others would act in the future.

Maria fit the diagnosis of a borderline personality disorder (BPD). Her relationships were unstable and chaotic, she was impulsive, and she experienced intense emotional reactions that seemed disproportionate to the event or situation.

Seventy-five percent of those diagnosed as BPD are female. Plus 75 percent of those diagnosed as BPD have been victims of childhood maltreatment, with a high percentage reporting sexual abuse. The experience of being sexually assaulted, especially before reaching puberty, sensitizes the child to sex before she is physically ready. The result is a vulnerable seductiveness and a stereotype of a borderline woman as irresistibly sexy.

My attraction to Maria was not sexual but very significant. My emotional responses to Maria are called *countertransference*. Analyzing the countertransference and reflecting on my reactions can provide important diagnostic information about Maria. If Maria affected me in a certain way, I can hypothesize that other people may feel the same. Using my knowledge of abusive men might give clues to why Maria continues to attract abusive men.

I wanted to rescue Maria. She told the group she had signed up for a vocational program (with support from social services) but had somehow failed to plan for money to buy textbooks. Maria described tortuous obstacles by not having the right books. She already had to deal with calls from the school about her children's learning and behavior problems. How could she have time to go to the school library to use their textbooks?

Maria was in a dilemma: I had to restrain myself from wanting to give her the $100. I could see other people jumping in to solve Maria's problems. Maria was like the wounded animal triggering a desire to protect and nurture. And I knew that the DV offenders, victims of their own abusive childhoods, often spoke of an initial desire to be the hero that saved the damsel in distress. The batterer could be initially attracted to Maria because of their own life traps. The conditional belief that "If I rescue her, she will love me and I can be happy."

Yet Maria was not an easy person to rescue. She was impulsive and resisted others' advice. Against all rationality, Maria signed up for the most challenging classes and the most credits possible. In her decision making, Maria took no consideration of the fact that she was a single mother still living with an abusive boyfriend (Maria had returned to her abuser but still was attending support group). How could this added pressure help her ability to succeed?

Maria was able to admit some irrationality to her behavioral choices and said, "I know it's too much, but that's the way it has to be." When I asked why, Maria said, "I have to push myself or else I'll end up failing."

Her reasoning was difficult to understand but was not going to change. Her life was all or nothing. Anyway, most of her behaviors were impulsive.

Planning the future seemed to hold anxiety for Maria. Maria expected the worst. She would rather jump into the pool without thinking about the possibility of rocks.

All the women in group advised Maria to take things easier, but she resisted. Her life trap was set in concrete. If a partner thought he could change Maria, he was going to be frustrated. Maria would resist any hero who tried to tell her what to do.

I wondered about Maria's boyfriend/abuser, Jeff. His level of physical violence was severe. Maria reported being thrown into glass windows and having her head jammed into the toilet. Once she told the group that Jeff had kicked her out of bed (she had to sleep on the couch) because she wouldn't sleep naked and/or have sex with him every day. What did this mean?

Jeff had been the victim of childhood trauma. Maria always wanted him to get therapy so he could follow through on his promises to stop his violence. For a while, Jeff received counseling from a woman pastor in Sun Prairie, adjacent to Madison. During this time, Maria's relationship with Jeff was positive.

Maria wanted Jeff to go back to this counselor, but he wouldn't tell her the pastor's name or church. He refused her pleas to go together to this therapist for couples counseling. He continued to be abusive, but she thought he might change again and be loving.

Maria's warmth was attractive to Jeff probably because he had coped with his childhood abuse by avoiding his feelings and dismissing his need for emotional connection. Many abusers spoke about a father who repeatedly told them, "Don't cry or I'll give you something to cry about." Crying and feeling sad were shameful.

Jeff was emotionally dependent on Maria. Jeff couldn't express his emotions. Maria emoted without effort. When Jeff felt aroused and irritable, he wanted her to comfort him. He got mad when she couldn't soothe him. As a survivor of childhood abuse, he never learned to soothe himself.

Steven Stosny, author of *Treating Attachment Abuse: A Compassionate Approach*, calls Jeff's concept of schema frustration *attachment anger.* Remember that losing attachment figures is like withdrawing from an addictive substance. When Jeff was physically or emotionally separated from Maria, his body craved the pleasure and reward neurochemicals associated with close proximity to an attachment object. He experienced attachment insecurity.

Anger helps Jeff cope with this attachment anxiety. The chemicals secreted in the brain during anger arousal—epinephrine and norepinephrine—are experienced like an amphetamine and an analgesic. Pain is numbed, and the body receives a burst of energy. For example, in football, when playing angry, athletes can win the game with broken bones and not feel anything until the game is over.

After the anger has passed, the individual feels depressed. The effect is physiological even if he kept from doing something he was ashamed of. In this addictive trap, he uses anger to avoid depression.

Attachment anger is also part of a child's normal initial response to separation from his mother. John Bowlby, founder of attachment theory, observed the reactions of children ages fifteen to thirty months in nurseries who were separated for the first time from their parents. He noted three distinct phases, which he called *protest, despair*, and *detachment*.

Bowlby's description of the phases are readily available and are often presented in his own words:

"In the initial phase [protest] the young child appears acutely distressed at having lost his mother and seeks to recapture her by the full exercise of his limited resources. He will often cry loudly, shake his cot, throw himself about, and look eagerly towards any sight or sound which might prove to be his missing mother. All his behavior suggests strong expectation that she will return."

All of the behaviors associated with the Protest phase of separation can be construed as angry. The child is "acting out" onto the world in order to produce return of his mother. In the protest phase as an adult, loud crying becomes yelling, shaking his cot turns into hitting the wall with his fist, and instead of throwing himself around, he throws an ashtray or breaks the TV.

Traditionally, males are associated with acting out and angry emotional/behavioral responses to trauma. Female adult survivors of childhood abuse typically internalize their anger into depression, anxiety, and self-hatred. More recently, the old rigid societal rules of gender are more fluid. In today's society, girl children are rewarded for assertiveness and athleticism. Instead of gender roles, the child's temperament, either active or passive, determines the individual's default coping style.

Many of the women adult survivors I met at PAVE surrendered to their schemas. As children, they learned to avoid abuse through people-pleasing and taking care of others. As adults, they became self-sacrificing out of guilt and submissive to authority from fear. Many fled from the subjugation relationship with their father into another one with their husband.

A victim personality exhibits a preoccupied attachment style. The mental model of self is negative; the model of others is positive. The victim takes the blame for things that go wrong even if they are not really her fault. The term *co-dependent* defines the victim's giving up her rights and identity within a relationship to meet the needs of others. Fear of abandonment also seems to drive a victim's difficulty in getting out of a violent relationship or returning to an abuser.

The schemas of the women's life traps are similar to the offenders: powerlessness, defectiveness, mistrust/abuse, abandonment, and emotional deprivation. Their patterns of coping are different. Offenders counterattack; victims surrender.

Maria did not fit the pattern of a traditional woman victim. Maria was tough and wanted everyone to know she did not depend on anyone. She could stand up for herself. As a teenager, Maria became the biggest, baddest girl on the street, instigating and winning fights against other girls. She also fought back against her abusive boyfriends, resisting control until his physical size and aggressiveness eventually overwhelmed her.

Maria believed in aggression until she came to PAVE five years ago. At the shelter, violence of any kind is not allowed. Residents were kicked out if they demonstrated aggression. The signs in the house read, "Hands are for helping, not hurting." The shelter was a safe house.

Maria said she stopped hitting her kids during her first stay at the shelter. Maria arrived as a terrible mother. Her kids ran wild and never listened to her. She'd scream at them saying, "Get out of my sight" and "I'll give you away to social services if you don't behave."

"Once I came to PAVE," Maria told the group, "I decided that I would not hit my kids. I wanted to be a better mother."

Maria described sitting Luke and Callie down to talk to them. She said, "I promised them I wouldn't hit them anymore. Luke didn't believe me and asked, 'Mommy, are you sure you are not going to hit us?'"

Maria leaned across the table as if she was bending down to look directly into a child's eyes. "I promise,' I said to them."

Maria sat back in dismay. "Then Luke started hitting me." Luke, as a second grader, had already been suspended from school for fighting and had been banned from the YMCA.

In the summer of 1999, I took off from work for two weeks to write a self-help book for inmates who were survivors of childhood abuse, trauma, or family dysfunction called *Lifetraps: A Workbook for Understanding and Change*. The Department of Corrections printed my manuscript into a paperback 9" × 11" book with a blue cover.

I translated Jeff Young's self-help book, *Re-inventing Your Life: How to Break Free from Negative Life Patterns and Feel Good Again* for a prison population. I needed to rewrite the book because his audience included people like me, neurotic and still unhappy in their lives. Those of us who coped with distress by internalizing. We make ourselves miserable.

The audience for my self-help book consisted of individuals who coped with problems by externalizing. They made others' lives miserable. Their lives were in total chaos. My readers were sitting in prison, sometimes in total isolation, with all the time they needed to figure out where they had made their mistakes. I wrote up instructional steps for the reader to follow in an analytical theorem.

I gave the life traps book to almost any inmate in my office who expressed even a little interest, and I sent over a large number to segregation. Some of the men I interviewed later complained to other inmates, "I went to her for help, and all she did was give me a book." But to me, self-help books were the key to understanding and change.

I bought all kinds of self-help books to loan out. One the offenders enjoyed was David Burn's *Feeling Good.* Burns explains the theory of cognitive behavior therapy. I could honestly recommend the book to the offenders because Burn's writing changed my life. I learned I could change my feelings.

Inmates have a lot of time to read and reflect. Some of the inmates reported reading their first book in prison. Looking back at the chaos in their life at the time of their offense, the offender has the space to link their adult problem behaviors with their childhood experiences.

Maria was currently in crisis. She had little time to reflect; probably no time to sit down and read a book. In addition, at PAVE, the women seemed to respond more to self-help books focused on feelings like Melody Beattie's *Co-dependent No More.* I tried to adapt the life traps materials to the women in the support group, but I never felt I was successful.

Most importantly, with Maria I did not want to suggest any blame or responsibility for her own victimization. The women at PAVE blamed themselves for their abuse as a child. And they blamed themselves for their current difficulties. I didn't know how to say, "You are not responsible for your childhood, but you are responsible for your adult behavioral decisions."

I wasn't the most tactful of people. I was also sensitive to their tendency to be self-critical and hate themselves. I didn't want to say the wrong thing and hurt the women more. After the group, after the glow of the emotional connection with the women had worn off, I would ruminate over my interactions with the women. I'd think about the group all week and cringe, thinking I unwittingly increased emotional pain.

One Thursday afternoon, at the end of summer, Maria called the shelter from her car in a panic attack. She was crying and talking incoherently into the phone. Terry, the staff advocate, could not understand her at first.

Finally, Maria calmed down a little. She was driving with her two children, who were sitting in the back seat. She had pulled off to the side of the road because she felt a tightening in her chest, feeling lightheaded, and everything felt unreal. Maria knew she needed help and called PAVE to help her through her meltdown. Terri asked Maria to use some relaxation techniques, breathing deeply and slowly, talking herself down to a calmer state. Maria did calm herself sufficiently to drive home.

Maria promised to attend support group later that evening. When Maria sat down at the table for group that evening, she was ready to tell a story, showing no signs of internal distress.

Maria threw a one-page flyer onto the table. She exaggerated a sense of outrage, sitting up straight and miming an attitude of shock. She picked the flyer up and started reading out loud. A local non-profit, *Clothes for Kids* (recycling children's clothes) was offering free school supplies.

"It's rude," Maria read from the handout. "'Please note. Bring back the clothes you received last year.' Isn't that rude?"

I laughed with everyone else because Maria was playing up her sense of indignity. She pouted, pranced, about in her chair, raising her chest with a sense of injustice.

I thought the directions on the flyer seemed more emotionally neutral. Wouldn't the charity need the clothes from last year to give to new children this year?

But Maria had already launched into the description of the events leading up to her emotional meltdown. "I went to the place. The kids needed the supplies. Their father wasn't helping at all, and Callie's teacher referred me." Maria expressed some shame at having to take charity but apparently had not seen any other option.

Maria said, "The kids and I stood in front of the building. There were two doors. I entered one, and as soon as I stepped inside, the lady told me I was at the wrong door."

"She [the charity lady] yelled at me, and then she yelled again when I went up to the wrong desk." Marie mimicked the charity lady sneering and speaking with disdain. Dramatically, she presented herself in direct opposition with sweetness and innocence. It was very comical.

Maria described the charity lady's attitude as superior, arrogant, and contemptuous. "She acted so superior. Like I was trying to get something over on her, that I was just lazy and really didn't deserve crap."

I was not familiar with this particular organization. I remembered an article in the Beaver Dam newspaper about a Mrs. Kay who originated the store and ran it by herself and her adult daughter. The article was complimentary, praising the woman for being so helpful to the less fortunate in the community.

I never met Mrs. Kay, but from Maria's unflattering description, I started to dislike her. I've met similar individuals who pitied the poor and hid their contempt with morality and self-righteousness. Maria was describing a person who was *shaming*.

Maria's stories inevitably included a plot twist when Maria momentarily considers using aggression to solve the problem of the moment. In this incident, Maria's first response to the charity lady involved anger. She told the group, "I wanted to hit her."

Maria flexed her right upper arm, showing a slight but definitely toned muscle. She exaggerated an aggressive stance and mimed the act of striking the sanctimonious bitch. Maria grinned.

"I really wanted to hit her, but I couldn't," Maria said. "I didn't want my kids to have a mother in prison." Again, I and everyone one else in the room avidly listening to Maria laughed. Each of us experienced a vicarious thrill of righteous anger and dominance. Maria was making fun of the fact that anger and aggression were physically rewarding. It was part of the human experience.

Her first option of aggression stymied, Maria was beside herself. She knew she had to do something to relieve an intolerable inner experience. She continued, "After we had gotten back to the car, I was so angry and needed to do something to show her. I told Luke and Callie we were going to take the clothes and school supplies back."

Then Maria spoke in a sad and pleading little boy's voice like Luke's, "'No, Mommy. Last year, when another boy didn't have school supplies, he was teased all year.'

"I didn't know what to do. So everyone buckled up and I started driving."

Maria was almost standing now. She was agitated, reliving the past moment. I was pulled to her and was in the scene beside her. She was driving down the two-lane highway, erratically. Crying, sobbing, and shaking. The children in the back seat were scared their mother's driving could get them killed.

Maria suddenly seemed to snap back into the present. She had more anger to share. She told us a story about Callie trying on new shoes. The charity lady's daughter was helping. The shoes were too small. Callie told her they hurt. "The snotty daughter kept trying to tell Callie that they were fine."

Then Maria tells us about the children picking out backpacks.

"To get a backpack, we went into a back room where the different kinds of backpacks were hanging on a wall. Callie looked them over and asked sweetly, 'Please, can I have the pink one?"

Everyone knew how sweet Callie could be. She was a beautiful child, with long, black hair and round, large eyes. While Luke was wild and unpredictable, Callie was always even-tempered and polite.

Maria went on, "Mrs. Kay barked at Callie, 'The colored backpacks are for older children. You have to pick one with a cartoon character.'" Maria became Mrs. Kay as an evil villainess who wanted to make children miserable.

Maria said, "Callie finally picked out a Minnie Mouse backpack and tried to look pleased." Marie showed us in her movement how she saw Callie: a child filled with disappointment, expressing the feeling of never getting what you want and always feeling a little deprived.

Maria ended the story with a description of what she did when she got home. Maria put on a fierce tiger mom face.

"I called the children's father and told him that he better get Callie the best backpack, whatever she wanted. That's when I felt better." Everyone laughed—we all nodded at Maria's efforts to make things right for Callie. That deadbeat dad should be held responsible for his child. Maria was right to demand he get off his ass and help out.

I finally interrupted Maria to point out, "After the phone call to PAVE, you felt better. But you didn't really feel good until you yelled at someone?" Maria tried all kinds of strategies to relieve her negative emotions; only verbal aggression helped.

"How does that fly with trying to be less violent?" I asked.

Maria laughed. I took a moment to explain to the group how aggression is physiologically gratifying but still is not always the best choice. They seemed to understand, but the consensus in the room maintained an acceptance of Maria's actions as justified and necessary. Women's power, taking control, was most important.

Aggression was being idealized, but I didn't comment. We were all laughing with Maria as she struggled with shame and humiliation triggered by the charity lady's demeaning behavior. The laughter and sharing were the healing mechanisms in play here. Maria's sense of defectiveness/shame dissipated during the confession process.

Laughing at oneself serves to distance oneself from the emotional experience. Laughing in a group provides the opportunity to move into a more objective perspective. Maria was transported from reexperiencing the shame to observing her shame with others. Hopefully, she also gained insight into her disorganized coping styles.

Maria's perception of the charity lady as humiliating was not questioned during the session. Later, I heard from one of my male DV group members that he had always seen Mrs. Kay as caring and giving. I entertained a few possibilities.

One possibility was that Mrs. Kay and her daughter were haughty bitches and only Maria was able to catch the charity lady's underlying implicit contempt; two, the male was more thankful and compliant than prickly Maria, resulting in Mrs. Kay's more pleasant behavior. The third possibility, and most plausible, is that Maria's overreaction to Mrs. Kay's behavior was part of her life trap.

Maria's coping responses to her childhood trauma were disorganized, impulsive, and ineffective. Hopefully she is learning a healthier, more effective coping strategy from her work in therapy. She already holds the best strategy for defusing shame: laughter.

CHAPTER 9

Ken and the Broken Mirror

I worked at Dodge Correctional Institution (DCI) from 1990 to 1995. DCI was a very busy and sometimes chaotic prison. Over three hundred male inmates a month, ages seventeen to ninety-nine, arrived at the Assessment and Evaluation Center (A&E) from county jails throughout the state. Many of those inmates were in psychological crisis. Some were new to the prison system and unable to cope, and others were extremely hardened, facing life sentences. Each stayed at DCI for usually no more than one to two months before being reassigned to a receiving institution, like Waupun Prison, a maximum, or Fox Lake, a medium-security institution with numerous vocational and academic (GED) programs.

One of my primary job duties at DCI was to complete a full psychological evaluation of inmates suspected of mental health or behavioral problems. I spent one to two hours in interviews with each referred inmate, examined the offender's social and psychological history, determined special needs and made recommendations for the best way to treat the inmate.

I liked the evaluation process. Each inmate was a jigsaw puzzle, each fascinating and challenging. Many of the inmates opened up to me and shared their life stories. The men often had huge files containing extensive information about his childhood, interviews with the victim and his family, of a man's social history including a description of the man's childhood, his educational and work history. Mothers were interviewed, criminal history was described, and his military status was obtained. I liked reading the reports and tried to develop a synthesis of his psychological profile throughout the years.

My interactions with the inmates were intense. DCI was run like an emergency hospital. Crises were common: many of the inmates had adjustment problems including violent outbursts, suicide attempts, and mental breakdowns. During a crisis I would be called to the man's unit, talk to the officers, and then the inmate. From this very limited information, I would have to make a decision regarding mental illness or safety. I had to think quickly. It was often exhausting, but I was never bored.

Since getting to know the inmates quickly was important to anticipate potential problems, each new man entering the institution was screened by a psychological services clinician.

In an interview of ten to twenty minutes, I completed a quick mental status evaluation, took a short social history, and if necessary, provided reassurance. Many of the men were traumatized, being thrust in a new, alien, and threatening environment. I needed to reassure them that their world had not ended. I repeated to each inmate, in different words and phrases but with the same message, "You can survive prison. You did bad things but you are not a bad person. Use this time to learn from your mistakes and you'll feel better when you get to a receiving institution. You'll be there for a while. You can start going to school or get involved in treatment programming and begin a routine. You can become a better person."

I was getting frustrated at the superficiality of my offender interaction and had decided to transfer to an institution providing therapy and treatment when I met Ken.

Ken, a slight thirty-five-year-old with long black hair and a suggestion of Native American ancestry in his cheekbones, entered the intake unit office and sat down, visibly distressed. I figured quickly that the interview would take more than ten minutes, and I motioned to the security officer that the twenty or so men already waiting for me should go back to their cells.

Ken's facial features were slightly skewed from normal. When he was happy and smiling, his features seemed more symmetrical and almost handsome. But in this first interview, his speech was pressured and his face filled with anger. He was outraged that he was in prison for doing pretty much the same assaultive behavior as his abuser. But his abuser was not in prison, and this was unfair.

In fact, his distress was so acute that tears came down Ken's cheeks as he answered my basic questions. Then he volunteered, "I've tried to commit suicide in the past. I've cut my wrists and taken pills."

My next question was, "Are you thinking about suicide now?"

Ken answered, "I always think of killing myself."

Despite the suicidal ideation, Ken denied any immediate plans or intent for suicide, so I did not request that he receive an observation placement. I provided my pep talk, coded Ken in the psychological clinical file with a major mental illness, MH-2, and gained Ken's assurance that he would do nothing to harm himself before we could meet in my office the next day.

For the next five weeks, I saw Ken every few days, or at least twice a week. I diagnosed Ken with major depressive disorder, noting than his depression was mixed with a high level of self-pity and anger.

When I shared my observations with Ken at our last session at DCI, he disagreed with my diagnosis of major depressive disorder. Ken told me, "I've been diagnosed with manic depressive disorder." Curiously, he insisted on this with an odd pride.

Now known as bipolar disorder, the diagnosis is associated with a chemical dysfunction in the brain which causes extreme mood changes, from depression to mania, or a state of extreme elation and high energy. The moods last a few days to years but are not associated with or correlate to changing life events. Bipolar disorder is seen today as largely genetic and carries fewer stigmas than other mental illnesses. Famous people like Abraham Lincoln, Vincent Van Gogh, and Patty Duke have been diagnosed with this disorder.

Ken demonstrated significant mood swings, but his moods were usually an overreaction to real or imagined life events. They usually lasted a few hours and rarely more than a day. Instead of mania, Ken experienced a mixture of irritability, dysphoria, and anxiety. I did not see him as manic-depressive; the moods were not being induced by a chemical imbalance in the brain and did not show any pattern. I believed his extreme mood changes and impulsive behaviors were a learned pattern—a personality disorder.

I diagnosed Ken's primary diagnosis as a very severe personality disorder with borderline, antisocial, and narcissistic features.

Personality disorder is the term used in *The Diagnostic and Statistical Manual of Mental Disorders* (DSM), published by the American Psychological Society. The concept of a personality disorder is the same as a life trap: both are defined as a pervasive pattern of thoughts, feelings, attitudes, and beliefs that significantly interferes with life functioning in different life spheres—interpersonal and vocational.

The DSM, now in its fifth edition, identifies ten different personality subtypes (borderline, antisocial, paranoid, etc.) and three clusters: odd or eccentric disorders; dramatic, emotional, or erratic disorders; and anxious or fearful disorders.

Ken fit the personality combination of cluster B: dramatic, emotional, erratic, and destructive behaviors. Borderline personalities are usually difficult to treat, are demanding of the clinician's time and attention, and are often seen as unpleasant. Cluster B is a mixture of the worst traits of the borderline, antisocial, narcissistic and histrionic personality.

Ken's character traits, which fit into the symptoms of borderline personality disorder, included his extreme mood swings, chronic feelings of emptiness, impulsive and self-destructive behavior, persistent, unstable sense of self, fear of abandonment, and periods of paranoia and loss of contact with reality.

A diagnosis of borderline personality disorder is common among adult survivors of childhood trauma. The victim internalizes the emotional pain of the trauma into depression, shame, and self-hatred. He develops an anxious/preoccupied attachment style. Borderline schemas include defectiveness/shame, powerlessness, and emotional deprivation.

Ken also had antisocial personality traits. Ken's history of being abused cemented his deep mistrust/abuse schema. I learned that Ken held grudges intensely, never forgiving anyone who had transgressed against him. Because of this, Ken presented with the typical chip on the shoulder and a chronic defensiveness.

Cluster B diagnosis includes histrionic personality disorder, personality traits that gave Ken his overly dramatic appearance. Ken lived in a world of crises, and everything to him meant the difference between life or death.

Ken's narcissism was atypical, unique, and difficult to describe. Narcissists are usually considered to be overinflated, grandiose, overt, thick-skinned, and preoccupied with fantasies of being successful, powerful, or beautiful. Ken did not fit into this definition.

Ken was a *fragile narcissist*. Underlying his sense of self-importance and superiority, Ken was actually deflated, thin-skinned, and shame prone. His arrogance and hubris counterattacked a very deep defectiveness schema.

Despite his inadequacies, Ken saw himself as special and spent great amounts of his time and energy in his inner world analyzing his thoughts, feelings, and behavior. He was articulate and could express his feelings and show insight into his difficulties. I thought that Ken would be a good treatment candidate. He was in crisis when I met him at DCI, and I felt frustrated that he was transferred to another institution. I wanted to start therapy with Ken right away.

One of the perks of being a correctional psychologist in the Wisconsin prison system was the ability to transfer to different prisons throughout the state. Each prison had its own atmosphere and focus. Fox Lake Correctional Institution was known for a more relaxed pace. The job duty of psychologists there focused on treatment rather than diagnosis.

After five and a half years at DCI, I transferred to clinical services department at FLCI in order to get deeper into my clients' personalities. Instead of just recommending treatment goals, I could help the offenders grow and change. At DCI, my encounters with the inmates were fly-bys, ships passing in the night, and intrinsically superficial.

At DCI, I had seen Ken every few days to monitor his adjustment and provide supportive therapy until three weeks later, when he transferred to Fox Lake prison. When I got to FLCI, I was assigned as his clinician. Since his arrival at FLCI a few months before, Ken had already been involved in conflicts with both staff and other inmates.

Ken was no longer overtly depressed or in crisis. I saw that a window of opportunity for therapeutic gain had passed. He had settled into a resistant pattern of victimhood and an external locus of control, a belief that other people and external circumstances determine his thoughts, feelings, and behaviors.

One of Ken's difficulties with his anger and aggression included problems with authority. This issue popped up quickly as a source of conflict early in my therapeutic work with Ken at FLCI.

Ken signed up for a voluntary ten-week small group therapy opportunity I was offering called Childhood Trauma.

The policies regarding the movement of prisoners attending any treatment group in the administration building required the inmate to report to the pass officer downstairs, sign in, show his ID, and be given permission to go up the stairs to the group room. For two years, there was a regular pass officer assigned, whom most people just called Riley.

Sergeant Riley was an angry and bitter thirty-eight-year-old woman, an unattractive and overweight individual who barked at everyone, staff as well as inmates. I tried to avoid her as much as possible; she scared me with her brusque and hostile attitude. With the inmates, Riley was relentless in making sure all rules were followed. Inmates were yelled at as soon as they entered the building to take off their hats or pull up their pants, tuck in their shirts, and only talk when questioned.

Sergeant Riley used her position of authority to bully those under her supervision. Most of the inmates secretly called her a bitch, and I had to admit (although not to the men) that I agreed with the label. Sergeant Riley showed no respect to the inmates and treated them as barely human.

Officers at FLCI could be typed into three categories in their attitudes toward inmates: (1) hard—enforce the institution's policies and procedures rigidly with the belief that inmates are always wrong; (2) soft—allow inmates to manipulate the rules; and (3) mellow—

treat all inmates with respect while judiciously adhering to rules and regulations, allowing for some flexibility.

Sergeant Riley was obviously the hard type of officer and admired by some of the staff, although she was disliked by all of the inmates. I had no control over how Riley treated the inmates and would be considered soft if I intervened on any specific inmate's behalf.

Most of the group members—six, including Ken—entered the group room for therapy, grumbling under their breaths about what a bitch Riley was. Despite this, they regularly took their seats in a timely manner, got out their class materials, and got ready for the group to start. Everyone did this but Ken.

Ken came into the classroom yelling and stomping, pushing tables and empty chairs, just aggressive enough to let everyone know how angry he was but not so disruptive that I would have to order him to be taken to segregation.

"Riley should treat me with respect!" Ken demanded. "She's trying to get me mad."

Ken could not see that Riley's mind-set, perspective, and priorities were different than his. He was egocentric. He expected others to know what he was thinking and feeling and to see situations in exactly the same way he did. His thinking involved psychic equivalence. He equated what he subjectively experienced via his thoughts, feelings, and beliefs with reality.

In many ways, Ken's responses to authority could be compared to a two-year-old who throws temper tantrums when he or she does not get exactly what is desired.

But Ken's egocentrism was different from a willful toddler, due to the effects of early childhood trauma, according to Dave Ziegler in *Traumatic Experience and the Brain*.

Ziegler wrote, "The healthy development of self-perception begins with egocentric importance, adjusts to allow others to be important as well and develops an interaction of bonding where the child expresses needs and a responsive care provider meets them."

But Ziegler noted that the initial stages of self-perception were different for children who experienced abuse and/or neglect. The egocentrism is not related to a sense of importance but to desperation: "The traumatized child has never felt like the center of the universe. To survive, he must make his needs and wants more important than anyone else's or he will finish last and in nature, the one who finishes last not only loses the race but may lose his life."

Ken demanded respect not from a sense of importance but of desperation. Disrespect is an important issue in prison and is the trigger for many of the inmate conflicts. What defined an action as being disrespectful in a prison? I asked Ken what he meant when he complained that Officer Riley was being disrespectful.

"She acts like I'm not important. I feel like a nothing, a zero. I'm exposed. Everyone knows that I'm crap."

"Where did you get the original idea that you weren't important or had no value?"

Ken shared a life full of bad luck, injustice, and rejection. He provided numerous examples of being emotionally abused.

Ken admitted to everyone, "I was born with hydrocephalus, water on the brain. I had lots of operations when I was little. I was partially deaf. I had a big head. My brothers and sisters picked on me a lot."

He went on to say that his siblings "made fun of me, called me names, whispered in each other's ears, talked quietly because they knew I could hear. Two, three, four of them would hound me all the time. They would poke at me until I finally got mad and reacted, and then I would be the one who got in trouble. The bullying never seemed to end. School was no better.

"My mother was an alcoholic. I remember coming home to see my mother passed out on the sofa, drunk as a skunk, so drunk she would lose control of her bladder. We had to constantly rotate the cushions on the couch. I can't stand the smell of urine. When I smell it, I get flashbacks and get into a sour mood."

Another memory provided more details of Ken's family life.

"I was sitting at the table for dinner, when all of a sudden, my dad turned and backhanded me in the face and I fell to the floor. He accused me of being disrespectful to my mother, when in fact it wasn't even me who said anything. I was always accused or blamed for stuff I never did or wasn't involved in."

Ken's one positive relationship as a child was with a special needs teacher who gave him individualized instruction once a week.

"She even kept coming to see me after I had changed schools," he recalled fondly. I could see Ken brighten as he shared his experiences with this teacher who gave him special attention.

An older male neighbor also provided attention and affection to Ken from the ages of ten to sixteen. Tragically, this neighbor took sexual advantage of Ken, whose emotional neediness made him vulnerable to a sexual predator. Ken's perpetrator was never arrested and thus went unpunished. As an adult, Ken felt shame and anger.

Ken liked to talk and enjoyed my attention as I listened to him share such a difficult childhood. He signed up for every one of the six childhood trauma groups I offered at FLCI during our nine years together.

Most of the groups were limited to terms of thirteen to sixteen weeks. Everyone started at the same time. There were no late arrivals or departures, and classes were highly structured with lessons and homework.

My last group with Ken was an open-ended process group that ran for two years. In psychological terms, process means that the group is unstructured with no designated topic for each session. After a brief check-in, the group members shared problems and issues of concern to them.

Ken was very active in group discussions and willingly brought up many of his difficulties with staff and inmates. Ken portrayed himself as the victim in every altercation and could only present his problem situations with an extremely distorted and rigid point of view.

Luckily, another group member, Dwayne, lived in Ken's unit and was able to provide collateral information and objective details, specifically how Ken often instigated the conflict. Dwayne was serving a life sentence for killing a man in a bar. He had used his prison time wisely, reading widely in Buddhism, and was the inmate leader for a self-help group. Dwayne volunteered for my life trap group to gain some insight into what led him to this point in his own life.

Ken came into group one day, angrily complaining about another inmate on the unit calling him a punk. Thirty inmates in one wing shared a communal bathroom and interacted in the day room, where tables were set up for the inmates to play cards, scrabble, chess or dominoes in small groups. Hot water was available for the men, as well as a microwave oven and an ice machine.

Ken said, "I was in the day room, standing in the line to get ice, and a guy I hardly know started flapping his mouth." Ken got agitated just talking about the incident which had occurred three days before.

"I wanted to hit him." Ken gestured aggressively while he recalled his thoughts and feelings from that moment.

Dwayne had been trying to help Ken get along on the unit and stay out of trouble. Ken really wanted to be Dwayne's friend and knew Dwayne was trying to help him avoid getting into so many conflicts. However, Ken often got angry at Dwayne for interfering in his life, reflecting a pattern of interpersonal relationships typical of a borderline personality, making a lasting friendship difficult.

It had been six years of working with Ken, individually and in group. And I had the small victory of hearing Ken verbalize what he should have done, though he did not do so.

"I should have ignored him, I know."

Dwayne asked him, "Why didn't you? The guy is a jerk. You know he tries to get into fights. He wants to show off."

"When anyone tries to intimidate or bully me, I automatically go into defense mode."

"But it's like you're challenging him to insult you," Dwayne noted. "The guy just wants to get a rise out of you."

Dwayne had provided an ideal route into Ken's past. I asked, "Can you think back to a similar childhood memory?"

Ken thought for a few moments. The group waited. Finally, he said, "I remember riding my bike one day and a group of kids came riding by. I stopped to cross the street, and this big kid came up to me and punched me. That kind of thing happened to me a lot."

"How do you think being bullied like that as a child affects you now?"

"I'm just waiting to attack and waiting for the confrontation to occur. I won't let anyone push me around ever."

Ken still had difficulty connecting his aggressive posture with the other inmate's verbal harassment. I was trying to get him to see how he was responsible. I didn't want to blame Ken for being insulted but to get him to appreciate that he was unnecessarily overreactive and his responses made the confrontation worse.

Some of Ken's overreaction originated in his belief that someone calling him a punk made him one. Although six years of therapy with me taught him a more rational response, he did not remember it in the moment of the crisis.

I prodded him, and Ken remembered the words I had said many times before. "What others say or do means nothing about my self-worth." I didn't know if Ken believed this.

Another crisis occurred when his unit officer, Officer Max, an attractive and pleasant female in her late twenties, assigned Ken to room with a particularly unpleasant inmate.

At FLCI, roommate assignments were made randomly unless tagged for security or mental health reasons as a "pair with care." Complaints about roommates comprised around 60 percent of interview requests to psychological services. Men in prison were not known for their social niceties. Many had poor hygiene, passed gas, or snored loudly.

The worst roommates were called Vikings, after the medieval Nordic seafarers who supposedly wore horned helmets and were known for their savagery and uncleanliness. This particular roommate didn't shower, stayed up all night talking, and acted like he was the only one in the cell.

Ken wrote me an inmate request slip that read, "Please see me soon" in capital letters with many exclamation points. Ken insisted that I use my power as a psychologist to get him a room change. Ken believed Officer Max had intentionally given him this bad roommate because she didn't like him.

He said, "She wants to make my life miserable."

The psychologists at FLCI were limited in affecting roommate changes. I explained to Ken that my power was, in fact, more limited than what most inmates believed. I only could encourage room changes when I thought the inmate was not safe in the cell. Ken just didn't like his assigned cellmate.

I told Ken, "I can only make changes when I believe there is a safety concern. If I let you out of the cell assignment, another inmate would have to suffer."

Ken insisted, in a threatening way, "I won't be able to stand it."

This argument didn't sway me. I said, "Remember Viktor Frankl, the Austrian psychiatrist who survived three years in a Nazi concentration camp during World War II?" Ken had read Frankl's book *Man's Search for Meaning*, and I quoted Frankl in my life trap materials.

Frankl wrote about inhumane camp conditions but noted, "Even though conditions such as lack of sleep, insufficient food and various mental stresses may suggest that the inmates were bound to react in certain ways, in the final analysis it became clear that the sort of person the prisoner became was the result of an inner decision ... what should become of him, mentally and spiritually."

I looked at Ken with compassion. But I presented the harsh reality discussed in Albert Ellis's Rational Emotive Therapy (RET), "You have two choices when faced with unpleasant reality: to be miserable or less miserable." I repeated my usual advice, "Accept the things you cannot change."

Ken understood such wisdom in the abstract but not when faced with the disagreeable situation. He continued to complain to me, both individually and in group.

I considered contacting the officer who made the decision. Ken had already claimed of the officer, "She hates me. She wants me to suffer. She knows that I will be miserable if I have to room with this slug." I doubted a malicious motivation for her decision. Officer Max was no Officer Riley. She was very friendly with me, shared information about the inmates living in her unit that would aid in helping them emotionally, and she expressed a desire to help the offenders.

But I was also aware that secretly, this officer, like others, might have been projecting an attitude that was smoke and mirrors. There were officers who did favors for undeserving but influential inmates. It was even possible that Max wanted to get back at Ken. I'm sure she didn't like Ken's whining and arguing whenever she gave an order on the unit. But I also saw another possibility: Officer Max could very well get angry if she felt I questioned her decisions. That could make it even more difficult for Ken.

I told Ken that I couldn't help him in his situation. I know Ken believed that I chose not to help him thus failing him as a support person in his life. I had said I cared, but in the end, he saw me just like everyone else in his life—someone who didn't care about him. He never expressed any anger toward me at the time, but I could see some resentment in his attitude that wasn't there before. He never stopped begging me to intervene.

But it was Officer Max whom Ken railed against, and in Ken's mind, she was a monster. Previous to this situation, Ken had liked Officer Max and had commented on her fairness. Now Ken only saw evil in her.

When Ken was railing and hating in my office, my focus shifted to Ken's face. His features, especially his mouth, became distorted, and his mouth seemed to move in slow motion, each word slurring and meaningless. In the second, I wondered if I might be witnessing evil.

I felt horrified at the ugly, uncontrolled nature of his animosity. But I pushed back my initial tendency to recoil and stayed with him. I was supportive even though I felt I couldn't fix the problem. Eventually, Ken gave up trying to convince me to intervene in his battle with the officer. He left my office that day, sadly no better than the day he had come in.

Anyone could see that Ken did not possess the necessary anger management skills needed to go to the officer and ask politely for a room change. Ken's emotions were too out of control to allow him to use such a social skill, one that the average person could easily master. In a move probably helpful to the functioning of the entire institution, Dwayne used his positive relationship with Officer Max and his respected position as a cooperative inmate to get her to place the undesirable roommate with someone else, giving Ken a more reasonable and socialized cellmate.

I don't know if Ken knew Dwayne had solved the problem for him. Dwayne's actions certainly made my life easier. It was difficult to get Ken to be rational, and I had difficulty explaining why Ken was acting so irrationally to the security staff. I always answered their questions with a "Ken sees the world in a different way." An uncaring cellmate probably would have overwhelmed his ability to cope, and no one wanted that. It would have been a problem for the whole institution.

Trying to explain and understand what was going on inside Ken's head, I found a psychoanalytical concept in my reading that seemed to apply, the *alien self.* This unacceptable sense of self as a result of the abuse is projected onto another person, usually an attachment figure. Alien self and projective identification are psychoanalytical terms introduced by Melanie Klein, who was a student of Sigmund Freud. In this defense mechanism of *projective identification*, the alien, unacceptable part of the self is unconsciously externalized onto another person, usually an attachment figure.

The concept of projective identification has been revived by Bateman and Fonagy in their new paradigm called *mentalization.* Linking cognitive theory with attachment theory, the model proposes that the child gains his sense of self from the caregiver-infant contingency, i.e., through the parent's reactions. The parent acts as a mirror. When caretakers react to the child negatively, the baby will identify with a bad sense of self, an alien self. While every childhood has some parental failures, everyone has aspects of the self that are alien or false, when parents are consistently negative, the alien self forms a structure that is experienced as evil/hateful.

The authors argue that ACES (adverse childhood experiences) rooted in traumatic experiences create unbearably painful emotional states in the adult survivor, leading to self-destructive behaviors. Externalization to another person of this alien self provides a way to reduce the unbearably painful emotional states and to feel righteously vindicated. The bad is in the other, not the self.

Ken vacillated between hating himself and suicidality with hating others and feeling aggressive. The part of himself filled with self-hatred was very open to therapeutic intervention. He listened to me intently and responded to a spiritual psychotherapy model I found in the *Course of Miracles.* The spiritual self-help approach was readily available in a book written for prison inmates called *Houses of Healing: A Prisoner's Guide to Inner Power and Freedom.* The author, Robin Casarjian, also wrote a series of videotapes that provide a ten-class course called *Emotional Awareness/Emotional Healing.* She has established the Lionheart Foundation with a goal of placing multiple copies of *Houses of Healing* in every prison library in America.

The psychological approach is cognitive-behavioral: one heals through forgiveness. Casarjian defines forgiveness (the miracle) as seeing the world is a different way.

"Forgiveness teaches us that under behavior that appears heartless, there is a soul of value. Forgiveness implies a willingness to accept responsibility for our perception, realizing that our perceptions are a choice and not an objective implies a willingness to accept responsibility for our perceptions, realizing that our perceptions are a choice and not an objective fact. Do you see just a jerk in front of you, or do you see someone who is wounded and insecure? In place of the angry woman or man you saw attacking you an hour ago, you may see a frustrated and scared little girl or boy."

Casarjian shares the affirmation, "Today I will see all anger (insensitivity, irritability, hostility, stupid behavior, etc.) as a call for acknowledgement, respect emotional safety, help, and love." Casarjian calls this process *forgiveness;* each individual needs to forgive himself as well as others.

"I am lovable and capable" is the affirmation to heal the anger and self-hatred. Loving the self is the antithesis of self-hatred. The concept appealed to my old hippie mind-set. "Desiderata," a 1952 poem by Max Ehrmann, could often be found on posters in the 1970s: "You are a child of the universe, no less than the trees and the stars; you have a right to be here."

My use of compassion and self-compassion as a therapeutic tool seemed to backfire in Ken. An antisocial twist to self-love had interrupted the gaining of a secure attachment—a positive self, positive others. He wanted me to read a nine-page letter he had written to his ex-wife whom he had abused. I thought it might say he was sorry for hurting her.

I lost my composure reading the letter. Ken talked about loving himself but used the idea aggressively by insisting that others, specifically the recipient of the letter, acknowledge Ken's lovability and specialness. Ken wrote a statement in the letter, a claim he often made: "I have a 170 IQ." I think the special education teacher assigned to Ken due to his deafness probably tried to boost his self-esteem by telling him how good he did on her tests. Ken was counterattacking his defectiveness schema with narcissism.

I thought I had created a monster. He had distorted the concept of self-love aggressively. "You better see how special I am." His ego was still threatened, and he responded in aggression.

Social psychologist Baumeister, in an article "Self-esteem, Narcissism, and Aggression," published in *SAGE Journal* (2000), summarized his research trying to confirm a traditional view that low self-esteem causes aggression. Baumeister notes that aggressive people often show high but unstable self-esteem. Violence occurs as a means of defending a highly favorable view of self against someone who seeks to undermine or discredit that view.

Self-love was the last thing Ken needed. But I had taught *self-worth*, not *self-esteem*. Self-esteem is often determined by positive versus negative traits. If I achieve a goal, I could add to the positive side. If I saw myself as attractive, I could feel better about myself.

Self-worth was the goal. Loving oneself simply for being alive. A famous psychologist, John Bradshaw, once said, "We are called *be-ins,* not *do-ers.* We don't *have to do anything* to be worth a life." Our behavior does not define our self-worth. What other people think does not define one's self-worth. Our worth is defined by the fact that we are alive.

I told Ken, "Even if no one loved you as a baby, you were still lovable."

"Even if the other children teased and bullied you, they were not right. They were stupid kids who wanted to put you down to make themselves feel good."

I told about Albert Ellis, a psychologist, who says we are all *fallible human beings*. People who make mistakes are still acceptable, still lovable.

"You can learn from your mistakes."

Ken's therapeutic progress was severely limited by his inability to accept making mistakes. He fought against admitting mistakes even when objectively he was the initiator of the problem. His shame was too high. It's difficult to learn from one's mistakes if one never makes any.

Ken finally shared the worst part of his childhood.

"My mother blamed me for her drinking. I was the reason she drank and then pissed on herself. She'd tell me that I was such a terrible kid. That I'd make her hit me because I had screwed up."

"So how do you think this affected you?" I asked. It's human nature to make meaning of our experiences. What belief about himself, others, and the world formed after repeated experiences from his mother? How did he cope with such rejection?

"I know it hurts to admit I'm wrong."

"And what would be so bad about being wrong?" I wanted to get at the deeper schema, the underlying core belief. "What would it mean about you?"

I don't remember exactly what Ken replied. His words expressed beliefs such as "No one would love me," "Others will reject me," or "I am unlovable."

My job with Ken became clear—he had to challenge the truthfulness of his beliefs. Could his mother have lied? Maybe she was rejecting him like she had been rejected by her mother or father?

This process needed to be repeated over nine years. His exposure to rejection had been consistent throughout his life, at home, in school, on the playground. This rejection from his mother drove deep into his psyche. His self-blame led to feelings of defectiveness and shame, which he attempted to counteract with hatred for others.

My group ended, and Ken started participating in offense-related treatment with another clinician. I saw him for monitoring every month or so, checking in on his progress. Almost every time I met with him, I could see progress. He seemed stronger emotionally and more insightful about how he may have contributed to a problem situation. After he started participating in a meditation program, he said it was easier to connect his feelings and thoughts and respond rationally.

Ken was released in November, and I retired from the prison system that next April. I had the opportunity to meet with him and ask his permission to write about him. I had seen him at a Stop Heroin rally when he told me that he was doing well on probation. When I started writing my book, he was the only offender I knew I could find and ask permission for me to use his confidential information.

I met Ken in a small coffee shop for lunch. At that time, he had been successfully on parole for two years and had passed two lie detector tests, proving he had been sober, actively participating in Alcoholics Anonymous groups and not breaking any parole rules. He also had been volunteering with a Stop Heroin community organization.

We sat across from each other in a café booth. Ken's back was to the wall, a common habit for former prison inmates. His hair was still long and fell into his face. He wore hearing aids in both ears.

I told him that I wanted to use him for the last chapter as a success case. He asked that certain details be changed so people could not identify him. He gave me permission to use his homework assignment found at the beginning of this book.

I wanted to know if I had helped him, how I had helped him, and what I could have done better: therapeutic closure. When I reminded Ken of the nasty roommate incident, he thought back to the time and laughed a little with some good-natured embarrassment.

"I hated you," he admitted. "I thought you were choosing not to help me. My thinking was really distorted. I even relapsed into using drugs for three months. I bought some pills from another inmate, crushed them up, and snorted them to get high. I didn't know what else to do with myself.

"Remember how I argued about your diagnosis?" he asked. "I didn't want to be called borderline. But now I am participating in DBT (dialectical behavior therapy), which was written for borderline personalities. So I guess I'm seeing what you were talking about."

Ken appreciated that he was doing good on parole, but still expressed anxieties; he was so afraid he would screw up by inadvertently breaking a rule and be sent back to prison. He told me that he was terrified to meet with an offense-related counselor from the parole office.

"He seems to believe that I'm always lying. That I'm trying to manipulate him in some way, getting away with breaking the rules, and he was soon going to find out what I had done wrong."

"You are a different person now. You can make good decisions about your behavior. Just keep doing what you know you need to do." I believed in a more supportive rather than confrontational approach. I wanted Ken to see how much progress he had made.

"I'm proud of you," I said.

These words seemed to be magic for him. He sat up straighter and seemed to lighten inside. I saw him relax and breathe. And I felt the reward of working with extremely emotionally damaged man— that joy of witnessing someone regaining a sense of his humanity.

Why do people hurt the ones they love? I argue that offenders are often adult survivors of childhood trauma who cope with emotional distress by externalizing, being angry, and using aggression. They survived their abuse, neglect, and dysfunctional childhood experiences by detaching from others, dismissing their feelings, and blaming others rather than themselves. They lack emotional intelligence skills and did not share the attachment experiences with significant others needed for true intimacy.

I have set out evidence to support this conclusion. I have provided statistical data, research, and theories. I have quoted brilliant scientists and philosophers to evidence the direct and causal relationship of early childhood attachment trauma to adult offending.

I have shared intimate details from therapy clients in their most vulnerable moments. I took care to change names, details, and dates, but I could not hide their basic personalities. The goal of my writing is to link what happened to the child to his essential character—what he believes, and the thoughts, feelings, beliefs, and fears that may have motivated his abusive behavior. I want every reader to see that these men did not deserve to be treated so terribly. They were victims before they were perpetrators.

I have also shared personal details and my own life traps in efforts to show that the reaction to adverse childhood experiences is universal. I internalized my emotional distress into anxiety and depression different from the offenders' externalization. I also shared my own journey to show that people can change maladaptive life patterns. Jeff Young's theory of personality development provides a vehicle to systematically analyze what went wrong and how to change it.

For myself, analyzing my own dysfunctional relationship pattern, I pushed myself to be comfortable with solitude. I learned to be less self-critical and trust that others will not reject me. I fought my attraction to emotionally distant romantic partners and realized that what I thought was love was merely attachment anxiety. I learned to love and feel love. I learned from my mistakes and broke out of my life trap.

My sensitivity to others' emotional pain never left me. I felt the inner distress and chaos of the offenders and victims strongly. I developed this compassion from my own childhood experiences. To be honest, the source of my maladaptive schemas and life trap was not just being isolated from my family in the hospital when I was barely a toddler. There was more. My father was emotionally abusive to my sister.

I loved my father, and he was a good man. He treated me like a princess. But he favored me over my older sister. He would criticize her and yell at her for making mistakes. She could never please him, and often, he just ignored her like she was not there. I would hear my father and sister arguing in the living room while I was down the hall in my bedroom, listening and crying. I was not abused but was witness to it. How did this affect me?

I developed ways to cope. When my father would start to get mad and erupt, I would smile to calm him down and try to be cute so that he would be distracted. Even now, when I see someone getting agitated, I smile nervously. In the prison setting, quite a few inmates got angrier because they thought I was laughing at them.

I grew up with the belief that I might be rejected like my sister if I was not sufficiently compliant and people pleasing. I carried these fears and anxieties into my relationships with boyfriends and lovers. It took much effort and perseverance to change these maladaptive patterns. My sister too was able to overcome her earlier difficulties; it helped that my father became more loving after he retired.

The negative effect on both me and my sister was fairly damaging despite the lack of any physical abuse or neglect. We both had only one ACE. Both of us survived and eventually thrived. Yet if this relatively little amount of trauma in my own fairly stable and supportive family was so destructive, how catastrophic would multiple and severe adverse childhood experiences be to the developing child?

Working with offenders and battered women, I found out how broken an individual can become if his emotional needs as a child are not met. Every child needs nurturing, comforting, and loving by his early caretakers. Without this secure attachment, the child is handicapped emotionally, socially, and psychologically. Some of the damage is irreversible, and any change is difficult and onerous.

Most of the men and women I met wanted to break out of their life traps. Most realized the self-defeating nature of their behaviors and were open to learning new ways to think about themselves and more loving ways to relate to others. Others were too impaired, and I was not able to provide the attention and support they needed to gain insight and change their lives. All of them presented with significant deficits in their emotional intelligence. These men and women were in need of special education psychologically, emotionally, and interpersonally.

The implication of the research is as follows: if society wants a responsible, emotionally healthy, high functioning adult citizen, it should better provide for each child's emotional developmental needs. These children fell through the cracks of our social services net. Treatment providers and concerned citizens are currently involved in a movement to publicize the ACES study, the devastating effect of trauma on a child, teach about resiliency, and demonstrate the importance of early intervention. I hoped that this book might advance their efforts.

The life trap treatment model I utilized avoids judgment, blame, and shame. Offenders were told, "You were not responsible for the abuse you suffered as a child. You did not deserve that suffering. But you are now responsible for how you respond to the abuse—for your thoughts, feelings, and behaviors."

There are other trauma informed curriculums that may also be helpful. However, trauma therapy with offenders should directly connect the childhood experience to the acts of aggression as well as other self-defeating behavioral patterns like drinking, using drugs, and excessive sexuality. A curriculum could be developed for victims also analyzing their own life traps.

Derek, in chapter two, repeatedly told me that he wanted me to write about his story. He hoped others could be spared all the pain he went through and the pain he, in turn inflicted on his loved ones. I hope so too.

People can change. Life traps can be healed. A secure attachment can be earned. Problem behavioral patterns can be corrected. What is necessary? The basic respect of every individual despite what they do or how they act: the behavior is the problem, not the person.

I have shared intimate details from therapy clients in their worst moments. I have done so worried about the breach in confidentiality because even if I took care to change names, details, and dates, the offender will be able to see himself in my writing. Yet I believe that the risk of sharing too much is overweighed by the potential gains of educating the public on the horrendous effects of childhood trauma.

An Introduction to Life Traps

How They Lead Us to Screw Up Our Lives and How to Change Them

Linda Nauth
Licensed Psychologist

February 2016

Based on the work of Jeffrey Young, PhD
Cognitive Therapy Center
120 East 57th Street, Suite 530
New York, NY 10022

Chapter 1
What Are Life Traps?

Life traps are patterns and habits of thinking, feeling and behaving that a person keeps repeating even though the habits are self-defeating and destructive. It's like "shooting yourself in the foot" or screwing up and doing something stupid just when you were close to achieving a long-time goal.

We can look at life like an obstacle course, with all kinds of barriers, stumbling blocks, and hurdles. Each of us tries to get to the finish line where we can reach our goals of being happy and feeling loved. However, some people seem to sail over these hurdles, avoid the pitfalls, and easily get to their goals. Others seem to keep falling into the same pitfalls over and over again. They keep running into traps and never get to the finish line, never feel happy or loved. Read the following poem. People with life traps get stuck in between the second and third chapter. They keep falling in the same hole, knowing it's there but falling in by habit.

Autobiography in Five Chapters (Poem)

1) I walk down the street.
   There is a deep hole in the sidewalk
   I fall in.
   I am lost … I am hopeless.
   It isn't my fault.
   It takes forever to find a way out.

2) I walk down the same street.
   There is a deep hole in the sidewalk.
   I pretend I don't see it.
   I fall in again.
   I can't believe I'm in the same place.
   But it isn't my fault.
   It still takes a long time to get out.

3) I walk down the same street.
   There is a deep hole in the sidewalk
   I see it is there.
   I still fall in … it's a habit.
   My eyes are open.
   I know where I am.
   It is *my* fault.
   I get out immediately.

4) I walk down the same street.
There is a deep hole in the sidewalk.
I walk around it.
I walk down the same street.
There is a deep hole in the sidewalk.
I walk around it.

5) I walk down another street.

Portia Nelson, 1993
From *There's a Hole in My Sidewalk*

More about Life Traps

Life traps are lifelong patterns or habits of thinking, feeling, and behaving that are self-defeating and destructive to others. Life traps begin in childhood and often help the child to survive in an unhealthy, dysfunctional environment. However, when these patterns continue into adulthood, they interfere in the individual's success and happiness.

Life traps keep us from achieving our goals. For example, Steve's goal is a nice relationship with his wife Melanie, but his life trap behaviors prevent him from achieving this goal. Life traps lead us to act in ways that we know are wrong yet somehow can't stop ourselves.

Steve loves his wife, Melanie. He was sure that they were made for each other and would be together forever. Yet sometimes he would yell at her for little, unimportant reasons. He would verbally abuse her and criticize her. He couldn't figure out why he was acting this way. He knew that his behavior was pushing her away, but he didn't know how to stop himself.

Life traps lead us to jump to conclusions, blow minor problems way out of proportion, and give us sensitive areas that people close to us can figure out and are then able to "push our buttons."

Lifetraps include the following:

1. *Core beliefs about oneself and the World.* The person develops these beliefs in childhood and accepts them without question. For example, a child may believe that he is "worthless" after hearing his father or mother repeatedly call him worthless.
2. *Emotional Pain.* The core beliefs are associated with painful feelings and memories.
3. *Behaviors.* People cope with the painful emotions associated with their core beliefs by many different kinds of behavior. These may change as the child grows to adulthood.

The life trap is named for its core belief. Dr. Jeffery Young is the psychologist who first figured out how destructive life traps are, and he identified eighteen different life traps. We are going to concentrate on five of the most basic ones.

1. Abandonment. The abandonment life trap involves your beliefs and expectations about relationships. With this life trap, you never feel safe in relationships; you might "jump into intimacy," so you will not feel so alone but then begin to push the loved one away when they get too close.
2. Mistrust/abuse. With the mistrust/abuse life trap, you expect that others will hurt or abuse you in some way. You believe that they will cheat, lie to, manipulate, humiliate, physically harm, or otherwise take advantage of you.
3. Defectiveness. With the defectiveness life trap, you feel flawed and defective. You believe that you are fundamentally unlovable. Anyone who gets close to you will not be able to love the "real you" and will reject you.
4. Emotional deprivation. With the emotional deprivation life trap, you believe that your emotional needs will not be met by others. These needs include nurturance, empathy, affection, protection, guidance, and caring from others.

You believe that no one truly cares for you or understands how you feel.

5. Powerlessness. With the powerlessness life trap, you believe that only one person can be in control. If you do not control others, you will be controlled and become powerless. You may see yourself as a helpless victim of a hostile world.

Many people have two, three, or even all five of these life traps. We will look at them more closely in later chapters.

Core Beliefs Distort How we See the World

Core beliefs are deeply entrenched beliefs about ourselves and how we relate to the world. Most people are not aware of them and usually are not aware of how they affect lives. Core beliefs distort how we see the world.

The core belief lens will highlight or magnify information that agrees with it and will minimize or deny information that contradicts it. For example, an individual who has a core belief that he or she is defective will not really listen to compliments or when given a compliment will dismiss it as unimportant or untrue.

A person's core belief can lead you to jump to conclusions, or lead you to overreact or blow a minor situation out of proportion. When someone pushes your buttons, they are triggering your core beliefs and the associated emotional pain. A core belief may also operate when you seem to react without thinking. Core beliefs can keep us repeating the same self-defeating behaviors even though you know that the consequences will be negative.

Here is an example of jumping to conclusions.

Situation   Core Belief   Thoughts

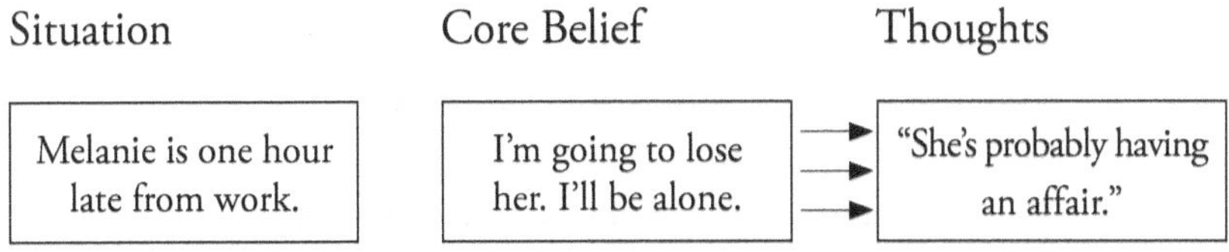

The unhealthy core belief of "I'll be alone" leads Steve to "interpret" Melanie's lateness in a way that involves her leaving him. The core belief that he will be alone and fear of the associated painful feeling of loss distorts his perceptions of Melanie and of their relationship. He jumps to the conclusion that she is having an affair without evidence.

Remember that jumping to conclusions, blowing a situation out of proportion, overreacting to specific situations, and having a "button" that others can push suggests that there is an unhealthy core belief and life trap operating.

Behavioral Coping Styles

Many people do not realize they have life traps because they do not want to feel the emotional pain associated with the unhealthy core belief. Some people will do anything they can to avoid or fight against feeling the emotional pain of their life trap. When the situation threatens to expose their unhealthy core belief, the person becomes stressed and learns to do *whatever it takes to feel better.*

Some people go to the opposite extreme of their core belief. Someone with a defectiveness life trap may criticize others so that they can feel good about themselves. He may act superior to others so that no one ever knows that he really feels worthless. This way of coping with the emotional pain associated with the unhealthy core belief is called counterattack.

Others may try to cover up the emotional pain caused by their unhealthy core belief. They may drink, take drugs, or use criminality to try to escape or avoid their emotional pain. Others may use appropriate behaviors such as working, having sex, or shopping but do these "compulsively." This means that instead of doing these behaviors as a choice when the time and place is appropriate, the person feels *driven* to these behaviors. They feel *forced* to work or shop or masturbate just to avoid feeling the emotional pain caused by their unhealthy core beliefs.

Others surrender to their core beliefs. For example, a person with a defectiveness life trap who sees himself as worthless may act in ways that maintain that self-image, like quit jobs or screw up in school just to prove that they are indeed worthless. These people feel the pain, but the pain feels familiar and more comfortable than changing their behavior.

Handout on Life Traps

Abandonment

This is the belief that you will be alone and that you will soon lose anyone who becomes close. You believe that close relationships will end sooner or later. The belief is associated with a feeling of overwhelming loneliness and loss. To avoid this feeling, you may cling to relationships and smother your partner or get angry when you sense someone is pulling away. You try to control others so they won't leave you. You may avoid close relationships and stay alone.

Mistrust/Abuse

This is the belief that others will hurt, abuse, humiliate, cheat, lie, manipulate, or take advantage of you. You believe that the harm is intentional. This may include the sense that you always end up being cheated or "getting the short end of the stick." You never let anyone get close to you or you form relationships with people who treat you badly. You may fight against this belief through anger and try to hurt others before they hurt you.

Defectiveness/Shame

This life trap involves the belief that you are defective, bad, unwanted, or inferior in some important way. Even if you feel acceptable outwardly, you feel *internally* flawed and ultimately *unlovable*. You are afraid to love. If others get close, they will realize that you are unacceptable and will withdraw from the relationship. To avoid the shame associated with this belief, you may flip to the other side of the "all-or-nothing" seesaw and act superior. However, you are sensitive to criticism and fear that if you have any faults, you must be worthless.

Emotional Deprivation

This is the belief that your primary emotional needs will never be met by others. These needs include nurturance, empathy, affection, protection, guidance, and caring from others. You feel like no one truly cares for you or understands how you feel. You feel *cheated*, and you alternate between feeling angry about it and feeling hurt and alone. You can flip to the other side of the "all-or-nothing" seesaw and feel entitled to take what you want. It's as if you are trying to fill the emotional emptiness inside you.

Powerlessness

This is the belief that you are powerless against others and vulnerable to their control. You set up a constant power struggle between you and others. It's you against the world. To avoid the feeling of powerlessness and helplessness associated with this belief, you may use anger and try to control others. You may have difficulty with authority figures, see them as trying to control you and doing the opposite just to prove you are in control.

Adapted with permission from Jeff Young, PhD
Copyright 1992
For more information, write: Cognitive Therapy Center of New York
120 E. 56th Street, New York, NY, 10022

Handout on Coping Style Behaviors

To cope with the emotional pain caused by the core belief, people develop behaviors that help them either avoid, counterattack, or give in.

Avoid or Escape "Coping" Behaviors

Addictions: Make yourself feel "good," at least in the short term, through addictions such as alcohol, drugs, overeating, excessive masturbation, etc. Avoid any emotional pain.

Withdrawal from others: Instead of being hurt by others, you stay away from them. See yourself as independent and self-reliant rather than wanting to be with others. Possibly retreat through excessive TV watching, reading, recreational computing, or solitary work.

Psychological withdrawal: Cope through dissociation, numbness, denial, fantasy, or other internal forms of psychological escape

Stimulation-seeking: Being alone and quiet means feeling the emotional pain of your life traps. Instead of feeling this pain, seek distraction from your feeling by the excitement of sex, gambling, risk-taking, compulsive spending, physical activity, trying anything new, etc.

Counterattack "Coping" Behaviors

Aggression, hostility: Instead of feeling bad, you make others feel bad by blaming, attacking, or criticizing them.

Dominate: Control others through *direct* ways to get what you want and avoid feeling helpless.

Recognition seeking, status seeking: Act superior; try to impress others by power, money, good job, great-looking girlfriend, etc.

Manipulation, exploitation: Hurt others first before they hurt you.

Passive-aggressive, rebellion: Give in to others' demands but do it "your way." Rebel in a passive way by procrastination, pouting, complaining, lateness, poor performance, etc.

Control freak: Maintains strict order, tight self-control, or high level of predictability through order and planning, excessive adherence to routine or ritual, or undue caution.

Surrender or "Give in" to the Pain "Coping" Behaviors

The pain feels unpleasant but comfortable. You keep acting the same way but hope that there is a different outcome.

People-pleasing. Maybe this time, others will love you.
Allow yourself to be controlled by others. It feels comfortable.
Keep trusting people. Maybe this time, they will not hurt you.
Put yourself down. It feels comfortable.

Adapted from Jeff Young, PhD. Copyright 1992
For more information, write:
Cognitive Therapy Center of New York
120 E. 56th Street, New York, NY, 10022

More about Life Traps

Abandonment Life Trap

The abandonment core belief is that you will lose the people you love and will be left emotionally isolated forever. You expect to be abandoned and to be alone *forever*. The emotionally painful feeling associated with this belief feels overwhelming as if you will not be able to survive without this relationship or loved one.

If you have an abandonment life trap, you will most likely have difficulties with intimacy and romantic relationship. Some people fear the feeling of loss so much that they avoid relationships altogether—trying to feel good about being a "loner" and independent from others. Others hate to be alone and will make sure they always have a relationship even if it means having more than one relationship at once, i.e., "having a spare. If one leaves, you'll have another one and will not be alone. Others may jump into intimacy too fast. Many domestic batterers try to control and isolate their partner to make sure the partner won't meet other people and leave.

Below is a list of different kinds of behaviors that people can use to surrender, avoid, or counterattack and help them cope with the emotional pain that their abandonment life trap brings.

Coping Styles in Relationships with the Abandonment Core Belief

Avoidance Behaviors

- Avoid relationships or getting close so you won't have to worry about them leaving. Fear of intimacy.
- Avoid being alone/jumping into relationships.
- Have multiple relationships, e.g., "Always having a spare."

Surrender Behaviors

- Intense relationships. Often roller coaster. Either wonderful or terrible.
- Difficulty accepting even temporary withdrawal or absence.
- High levels of jealousy. You assume that your partner will cheat or leave.
- Dependency and obsessiveness about the relationship. "Can't live without partner."

Counterattack Behaviors

Be possessive and controlling to make sure she won't leave.

Defectiveness Life Trap

A fear that others will discover our defectiveness can also make intimacy difficult. Below, a batterer discusses his mix of abandonment and defectiveness life trap and how both complicated his desire for intimacy.

> Since I really felt myself to be inadequate, unreliable and generally no good, how in the world could I be comfortable about someone really getting to know who and what I was? At the same time, my self-imposed isolation required me to alleviate my loneliness. I was caught between a rock and a hard place, fearing disclosure of my failings and fearing the destructive effects of loneliness. When the loneliness became unbearable, I would seek the intimacy and the feeling of loneliness would lessen. As the fear of loneliness became less acute the fear of disclosure became more intense until this in turn became unbearable. I would then start isolating myself in order to lessen that fear.
>
> This was all pretty difficult for the people who loved me to understand. Not being privy to the powerful emotions which were motivating me, all they could see was that I was alternately affectionate and distant, interested and apathetic, loving and cold. It must have seemed to them that sometimes I loved them and sometimes I didn't. What they were most aware of was that I was rejecting the intimacy I had previously sought.
>
> A batterer's perspective by Michael Wicks

Defectiveness is probably the most common life trap in offenders. Many won't allow themselves to feel defective and attempt to counterattack with a front of superiority and overly high self-esteem. However, this front is very fragile—anyone can "disrespect" you and threaten to expose your unworthiness.

The defectiveness life trap is often developed in childhood when a parent consistently shames the child, is verbally abusive, and/or punishes in a way that suggest the whole child rather than the specific behavior is "bad." The child develops the belief that he or she is "bad," shameful, and unlovable.

Coping Styles in Relationships with the Defectiveness/Shame Core Belief

Avoidance Behaviors

You don't get close to others to keep them from seeing the hidden, shameful parts of you. There's always the sense that "If others really knew you, they wouldn't be able to love you."

Numerous or a series of short-term, superficial relationships. These make you feel better temporarily but no one gets to know the real you.

Counterattack Behaviors

Use anger to cover up the feelings of shame through the "shame-rage" spiral. Blame others as cause of negative events, thereby avoiding personal responsibility experienced as shameful.

May be abusive, critical or neglecting of partner. "If I put you down, I feel better."

May be perfectionist. Any flaw suggests defectiveness in "all-or-nothing" thinking.

Seek a "trophy" wife who others will admire and see you with respect for attracting her.

Idealize your partner. The higher her value, the higher your value. (Initial idealization changes as time goes on, when you begin to devalue the partner, spotting every little flaw or imperfection.

Every flaw in your partner means reflects poorly on you and means you are defective.)

Be a "player." A lot of women admiring you is better than only one.

Overly sensitive to "put-downs" and being "disrespected."

Mistrust/Abuse Life Trap

With this life trap, you believe that all people will hurt, betray, and use you. Intimate relationships are potential traps—those closest to you can hurt you even more, so it's safer to keep people at a distance. You have to be on your guard at all times since you assume that even if someone is nice at the moment, they will soon turn on you and try to hurt you.

Those with the mistrust/abuse life trap often have poorly defined "boundaries." There is an invisible shield surrounding us like a wall or capsule. This invisible line marks our limits—where we end and the rest of the world begins. This line or wall is called a boundary and defines who and what we are. People can build too strong a boundary or shield and end up feeling isolated, alone, and lonely. Thus while it is important to build a boundary to define ourselves, we must also be able to connect with others. One way to visualize this is as having a zipper on the inside of the shield. It can be unzipped for closeness or zipped tight for protection and withdrawal.

People with a mistrust/abuse life trap oftentimes have never been able to develop a positive boundary. A healthy boundary is developed when others in your world respect you for who you are, respect your feelings, and do not try to force you to be what they want you to be. If you grew up in a dysfunctional family, there may have been assaults on your boundaries including incest, physical abuse, or overly controlling parenting. You start to believe that you can never trust others not to invade your boundaries.

Coping Styles in Relationships with the Mistrust/Abuse Core Belief

Avoidance Behaviors

- Don't get close to others.
- Worry if you share yourself it will be used against you.
- People cannot be trusted.

Counterattack Behaviors

- Respond with anger and violence when others are perceived as "hurting you."
- Attack first to avoid getting hurt. Attack to get revenge or "payback" for those who may hurt you.
- Sadistic/cruel side. You feel satisfaction when you hurt others.

Emotional Deprivation Life Trap

This life trap is the most difficult to identify. It is experienced as a lack of something—a lack of getting what we want, of feeling deprived, of feeling empty inside. A child might develop this unhealthy core belief "I'll never get the love I need" by having a childhood with a high level of parental neglect.

Coping Behaviors in Relationships with the Emotional Deprivation Core Belief

- Can't soothe self (make oneself feel good) when stressed without using external tension-reducing behaviors (i.e., substance abuse, violence, etc., that distract, numb, or reduce painful feelings.)
- Expectation that partner will "make you feel better" and meet all your emotional needs.

- Don't communicate thoughts, feelings, or need and then feel disappointed or angry when you don't get what you want.
- Feel empty inside.
- Experience distress when your partner pays attention to others (e.g., baby, family members, etc.). "All or nothing" thinking leads to the belief that if you do not get "all of her love and attention," then you will get none. Feel cheated, unloved, deprived, and envious.
- Counterattack with demanding and entitled behavior.

Powerlessness Life Trap

Offenders don't often experience the emotional pain associated with this life trap. They often counterattack to avoid the feeling of powerlessness and try to control others. If you can feel powerful, you can avoid feeling powerless. This is part of the "all-or-nothing" thinking that makes up unhealthy core beliefs, and we will discuss this later. Unfortunately, one of the ways to temporarily feel powerful is to hurt others. Manipulating others, making them feel bad by verbally abusing them, seeking revenge, or physically hurting them can bring about a temporary feeling of "satisfaction." This counterattack behavioral style is very dangerous, and you need to seek help if this is a pattern you have developed. Please seek help for this life trap.

One way an individual could develop this core belief is by experiencing abuse as a child or watching parental violence. As a child, one is indeed powerless and cannot stop the violence. It is emotionally painful to witness or experience violence and not be able to stop it.

Coping Behaviors in Relationships with the Powerlessness Core Belief

Surrender Behaviors

- Give in to the demands of others.
- Choose controlling partners who cannot tolerate your disagreement, opinions, independence, or paying attention to your own needs

- Take care of others at expense of self

Counterattack Behaviors

- Rebel against rules and authority
- Become controlling of a partner by forcing her to meet your physical, emotional, and sexual needs without thought for her own needs.
- Verbal abuse to affect an emotional response from partner.
- "Don Juan" syndrome. Exert effect on women by seducing them but then withdrawing (due to fear of intimacy/abandonment).
- Experience "satisfaction" when violent. Violence may temporarily transform feelings of weakness into powerfulness with the belief that one has control over the other person.
- Changing life traps.

Usually, when people try to change, they focus on changing their behavior. But remember, life traps are more than just behavior. They include the following:

- Unhealthy core beliefs about oneself and the world.
- Emotional pain. The core beliefs are associated with painful feelings and memories.
- Behaviors. Life trap behaviors are the ways that people cope with the painful emotions associated with their core beliefs.

Let's use the How People Think Determines How They Act cycle to look more closely at the full cycle of core beliefs, emotional pain, and behaviors of a life trap. Remember, thoughts and beliefs lead to feelings, which lead to behaviors, which then lead to short-term and long-term consequences.

How People Think Determines How They Act

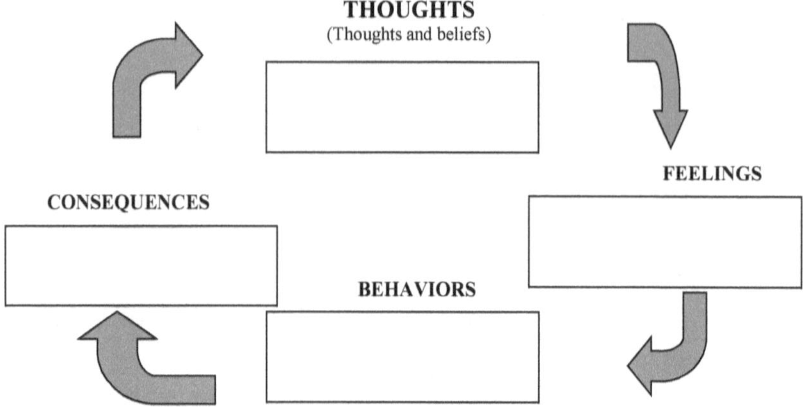

Let us look at an example of Carlos. Carlos believes that "a real man" never lets someone insult him. One night in a bar, a drunk spills beer over Carlos when he is with a new girlfriend. Carlos sees this as an insult. He hits the drunk and ends up in jail.

How We Think Determines How We Act

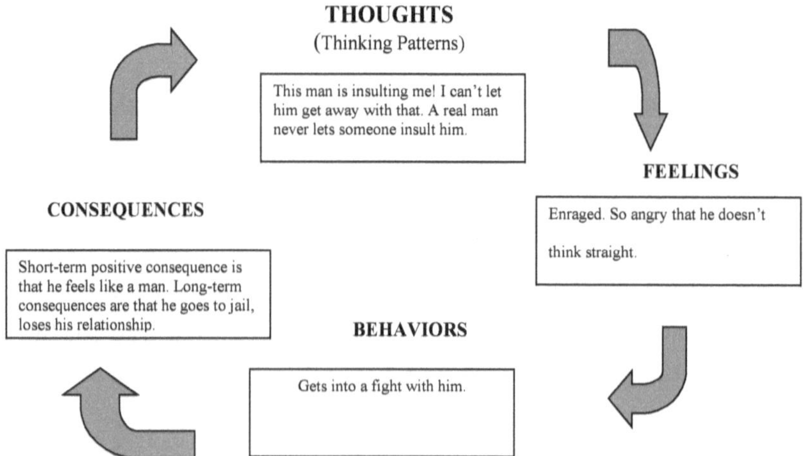

The importance of changing your *thoughts and beliefs*.

Carlos doesn't like the long-term negative consequences of his fighting and decides to stop fighting. He decides that he will stop and think of the consequences of his behaviors and *will not fight.*

How People Think Determines How They Act

Carlos's Example
Change Pattern No. 1

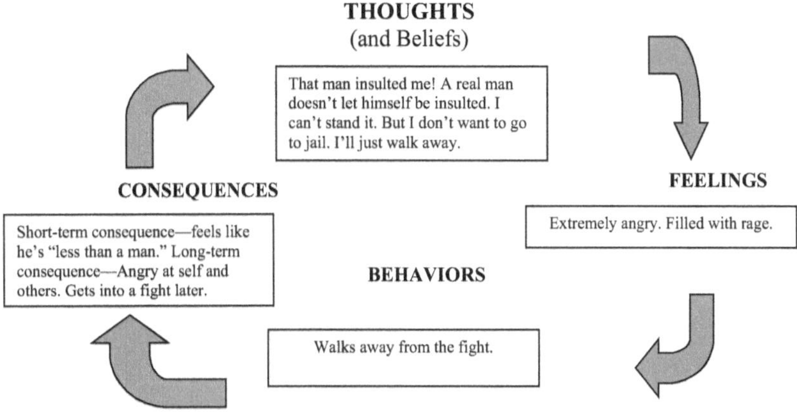

In this example, we see that Carlos can change his behaviors if he sees that they will lead to consequences he doesn't like. Carlos can walk away from the drunk because he knows he will end up in jail if he gets caught hitting someone. But he is still angry from believing that the man insulted him. He also feels bad about himself because he thinks that he allowed someone to insult him. He sees himself as "less than a man." Carlos still feels angry and now feels bad about himself. Although he walks away from this fight, he gets into another fight later in the evening.

This example helps us understand that while it is somewhat helpful for Carlos to problem-solve, see the negative consequences of fighting and change his behavior from fighting to walking away, it is more important for Carlos to change his thinking. He has to "challenge" his beliefs:

1. The man did indeed insult him.
2. Someone insulting him makes him "less than a man."
3. That he "can't stand" being insulted.

We have to understand that just because we have a belief, our belief may not be true or helpful. Carlos thought he was being insulted. He had a belief that he would not be a "real man" if he was insulted and did not fight, and finally, he believed that fighting was necessary and important. However, these beliefs may not be true or helpful to Carlos.

Carlos needs to examine and challenge his beliefs:

Is it true that the drunk was insulting him? Maybe the drunk was just being a drunk and spilled beer on him by accident.

Is it true that a "real man" has to fight when he is insulted? Maybe a "real man" is someone who is home to take care of his son. By walking away, Carlos avoids trouble and goes home to his son. His son loves him and thinks Carlos is a "real man" to be there to spend time with him.

Does another person's action "control" Carlos? Someone pushes a button with an insult to Carlos and he fights. This does not have to be true. Carlos can decide in the situation if the insult deserves such a drastic response.

Carlos's girlfriend may think Carlos should fight, but she may not really care about Carlos much. She just wants a big spender to show her a good time. Carlos might be more of a "real man" if he dumped her and went home to be with his wife.

Carlos knows that his mother is getting old and will need him to help her out. She might get sick and die. Carlos knows that he doesn't want to be in jail when she is sick and needs him.

Is it true that Carlos "can't stand" it if someone insults him? No, if Carlos chooses to stand it, he can cope with the unpleasant reality that some people do not always act the way we want them to.

In addition to challenging these beliefs, Carlos must challenge and change his core beliefs:

As Carlos grew up, his father was abusive and insulting. Carlos developed a core belief of himself as *powerless* to stop someone from abusing him.

Carlos's father called him "worthless" and "good for nothing." Carlos's core belief is that he is worthless and good for nothing and feels shame. He counterattacks this core belief by acting like a big shot and a "player." However, he is overly sensitive to anyone "disrespecting him." If anyone disrespects him, he feels the shame of his defectiveness core belief.

Carlos's example pattern no. 2. Here he challenges and changes his beliefs about whether an insult makes him "less than a man." He decides that his worth as a person is not changed by the words or behavior of an intoxicated man.

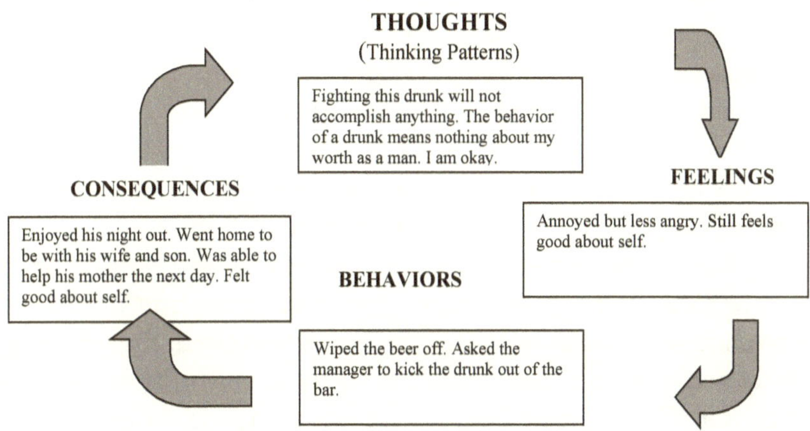

Carlos changed his belief that the drunk's behavior equaled an insult. He can also change his beliefs about what he needs to do to be a "real man." Most importantly, he started to change his core belief that he was powerless and defective. He realized that now he is no longer a helpless child but a man who can decide whether a drunk's behavior is worth going to jail. He also understands that he is not defective. He sees that his father had his own life traps and tried to shame Carlos to make himself feel better. If he can change his thinking, then he will be able to walk away easily and go about his business. He will avoid the problem behavior and will avoid the negative consequences of going to jail. He will also feel good about himself and make it less likely that he will get in a fight in the future.

In summary, we can make changes at any point in the cycle if we do not like the consequences we achieve. We can change our behaviors. We can calm ourselves by using relaxation and stress management skills. However, a very important place to change our life traps is to change our thoughts, beliefs, and core beliefs.

Challenging and Changing Unhealthy Core Beliefs

It is difficult for anyone to change core beliefs about others, the world, and ourselves. The difficulty is understandable when one learns that core beliefs are usually developed in childhood often before an individual learns to speak and before he or she has any memories of life. Even before a child learns language, the child learns to organize the world and develops beliefs about how the world is, how others are, and how he or she is. The child forms beliefs about whether the world is a friendly place, whether others can be trusted, whether he or she is a worthwhile individual.

When a child develops his core beliefs in a negative and abusive environment, the core beliefs become maladaptive and unhealthy. The child develops beliefs that others can't be trusted, that his emotional needs won't be met, or that he or she is unworthy of love and attention. These core beliefs then act like a lens and distort how he organizes new information. His distorted core beliefs and emotional pain lead to life traps.

Even when a child grows up in a loving and caring environment, there are many ways in which a child can still develop unhealthy core beliefs. Research studies of children have found that young children do not have fully developed thinking skills. A child is not capable of flexible, mature thinking and even in the best environment can develop unhealthy core beliefs.

A famous French psychologist, Jean Piaget, studied children as they grew and noticed that children viewed the world differently from adults and could not think in a flexible or balanced way.

Children have difficulty seeing the world from other people's perspectives. If a father promises a six-year-old they will go to a baseball game and the father is not able to go, then the child may think the father refused to go. The child figures that from his own point of view, the father must not love him or want to be with him. One offender I knew had a terminally ill younger brother. The parents were, of course, very focused on the child who was sick, but that did not mean they did not care about the older child. However, the offender as a child only knew that he was not getting the love he wanted. He could only see the situation from his own perspective. He developed the belief that he was not loved.

Thus, when we look at how core beliefs and life traps develop, our focus is not on exactly the reality of what happened to the child. We look at how the child saw his world. What messages did the child organized from his experiences? What beliefs did he develop about himself, his world, and others? We look at what the events and actions of other people "meant" to the child.

Children also tend to think in rigid, extreme ways. In one study, children are told of two boys: one boy deliberately breaks one of his mother's expensive china cups, but the other boy accidentally breaks six of the china cups when he tries to serve coffee to his mother and a friend. At age six or seven, children almost always see the boy who breaks six cups by accident to be more evil than the child who broke one cup on purpose. At this age, the children could only focus on one part of the story, i.e., the number of china cups that were broken. The child's thinking at the time that he is developing core beliefs is by its very nature inflexible, extreme, and rigid.

Children use very rigid, "all-or-nothing" thinking. Their all-or-nothing thinking leads to beliefs that are believed to be true, completely true, always true, and true for the rest of eternity. This is the nature of life trap core beliefs: rigid, unconditional, and seemingly unchangeable.

For example, as a child, his father tells Carlos that he is "worth-less." Carlos believes his father and does not question whether his father could be mistaken. As an adult we can see that Carlos's father was indeed mistaken. As a child, Carlos was born by nature precious and lovable. His father had his own life traps. However, Carlos believed his father, and because of Carlos's "all-or-nothing" thinking style, his belief "I am worthless" has the following qualities:

"All-or-nothing:" Carlos sees himself as completely worthless. There is not a drop of anything worthwhile in him according to this belief.

Unconditional. The belief "I am worthless" is unconditional. There is no condition under which Carlos could be worthwhile. The statement is not "I'm worthless if I screw up" or "I'm worthless if I lose my job" but "I am always worthless."

Unchangeable: There seems to be nothing Carlos can do to change his worthlessness. His defectiveness seems true and will never change.

Carlos needs to challenge his "all-or-nothing" thinking. He can develop a more balanced way to look at himself and his world. One way to look at qualities in a more realistic way is to see them on a continuum. A continuum is a scale ranging in degrees like heat. We start very, very cold and then less cold to neutral, then to warm, very warm, and hot.

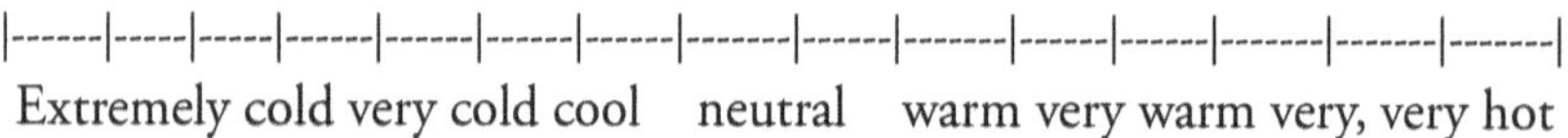

|-----|-----|-----|------|------|------|------|-------|------|-------|------|------|-------|-------|-------|
 Extremely cold very cold cool   neutral   warm very warm very, very hot

In all-or-nothing thinking, you see the world in extremes of the continuum. Things are black or white, perfect or worthless, beautiful or ugly, etc. People are perfectly good or terribly bad, wonderful, or horrible. Unhealthy core beliefs are not realistic; healthy alternative beliefs are flexible and balanced.

Flipping on the "All-or-Nothing" Seesaw

All-or-nothing thinking forms the basis of distorted core beliefs. Thus for each core belief, the individual usually picks an extreme position on a continuum. Let's look at some of the life trap core beliefs again at and see how the different beliefs can be put on a continuum or what I call a "core belief seesaw." I call it a seesaw because people "flip" from one end of the seesaw to the other. Their all-or-nothing thinking keeps them at either end instead of the balanced middle.

Finding Balanced Beliefs

Balanced beliefs are flexible, that is, they take different factors and circumstances into account. Balanced beliefs are not extreme, that is, they do not use "all-or-nothing" thinking. Balanced beliefs are flexible, not rigid, and show the world and the people in the world as changing and with the "ability to change." Balanced beliefs help you to:

Develop a positive identity—an understanding and good feeling about who you are

Develop boundaries between yourself and other so that you can be open with others yet set limits with them and teach others to treat you with respect

Learn how to experience true and healthy intimacy with others.

Abandonment "All-or-Nothing" Seesaw

Two together as one

Alone

Two Together as One

Example: Steve originally avoided his core belief that "I'll always be alone" by dating many women but never becoming emotionally close with any of them. When he met Melanie, he was able to connect with her emotionally. However, he then became so worried that she might leave the relationship and leave him "alone" again that he counterattacked by attaching himself completely to her so that they would become "two together as one." Steve believed that a relationship is made up of two half people becoming *whole* together.

Every time that Melanie showed independence, Steve became fearful that she would leave him and he would feel the pain of his abandonment core belief. So he would flip-flop to the other side of the all-or-nothing seesaw by trying to control Melanie and demand that she lose her own identity and become "one with him."

When Melanie finally left Steve, he became obsessed with her. He believed that his life was not worth living without her [like many romantic songs suggest] and began stalking her. He was still counterattacking his belief and avoiding the painful feeling that he was "alone."

Balanced Beliefs about Abandonment

Abandonment involves the belief that you will be totally alone and isolated without any ability to connect with others. The truth is that we are alone in a sense that human beings are in their own body and are born and die alone. While this sounds pretty depressing, it is a part of the human condition—we are all in some sense alone.

Yet while in one sense we are each alone, we still can connect emotionally with others. However, it is unhealthy to want to lose our sense of aloneness by simply melting into a relationship. To connect emotionally in a meaningful way, you must learn to be by yourself—and enjoy it. You must become an individual, a unique and special person who has his or her own sense of self and identity.

Without your own sense of self, you become desperately fearful of being alone and actually can become "addicted" to other people. Popular culture maintains the idea that we are nothing without someone to love and the concept that losing a loved one is like drug withdrawal. While this author is certainly not demeaning the idea of romantic love, as well as the understanding of the sadness and grief of losing a loved one, it seems noteworthy to stress the importance of individuality within relationships.

When two people fall in love, two people suddenly let the walls between them fall and feel close, feel as one, and it is so exhilarating and exciting that nothing else can compare. It is as if each loses their individual personality in the other. Some fear this process; some seek it out and go from relationship to relationship just to experience the joy and release of losing themselves in another.

Tony Kubicki, a social worker from Milwaukee who works with domestically violent men, describes the process:

"Every romantic relationship starts with a kind of symbiosis or merger in which the partners believe they are divinely matched and on the same wavelength in every way. Eventually, the glow wears off and differences begin cropping up ..."

The awareness of differences between the two, the awareness that each is a separate person is a painful reminder of the loss suffered as a child by the person with the abandonment core belief. The awareness of differences between two people reminds them of the feeling of overwhelming loss and aloneness.

In a violent relationship, the victim attempts to avoid the feeling of aloneness through attempts to merge her personality with the abuser. She escapes from the unbearable feeling of aloneness by becoming one with the abuser—he tells her what to do and what to think and she is part of him. The same thing can be seen outside of an intimate relationship through the joining of a cult or gang. The individual becomes a part of a greater whole and escapes his aloneness by loss of his/her individuality and feeling of separateness.

A person who counterattacks his sense of aloneness seeks to make another person part of himself. In an intimate relationship, he seeks to dominate the other person and include their personality into his own. He thinks he needs the other person to make him feel whole. Both individuals depend on each other to help them avoid their sense of abandonment and aloneness.

Achieving a feeling of connection, a sense of intimacy, is a natural and beautiful human goal. Intimacy, however, is not a losing of oneself in another but rather transcending oneself with someone or something outside oneself. This may be done through the love of another person, through the creative process, through nature or spirituality. Falling in love is an experience; staying in love is an art, a skill that involves maintaining one's own separateness and yet going beyond one's self to touch another. One needs self-love first, self-love for oneself as a unique and beautiful human being.

Kahlil Gibran in *The Prophet* proposes a balanced and healthy view of intimacy:

> Let there be spaces in your togetherness,
> and let the winds of the heavens dance between you.
> Love one another but make not a bond of love:
> Let it rather be a moving sea between the shores of your souls.
> Fill each other's cup but drink not from one cup.
> Give one another of your bread but eat not from the same loaf.
> Sing and dance together and be joyous, but let each one of you be alone.
> Even as the strings of a lute are alone though they quiver with the same music.

Abandonment All-or-Nothing Seesaw with Balanced Middle

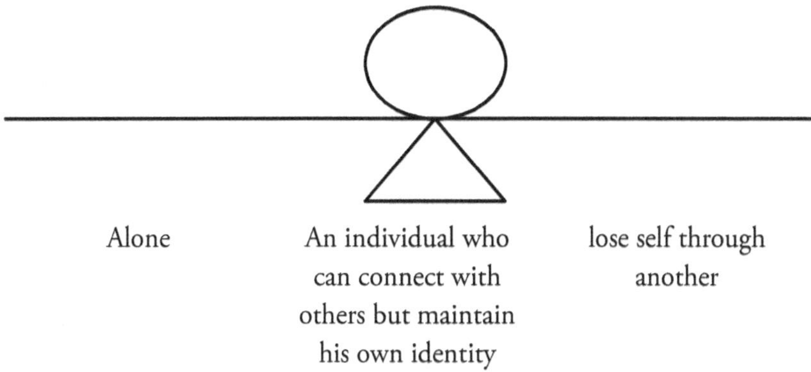

Defectiveness "All-or-Nothing" Seesaw

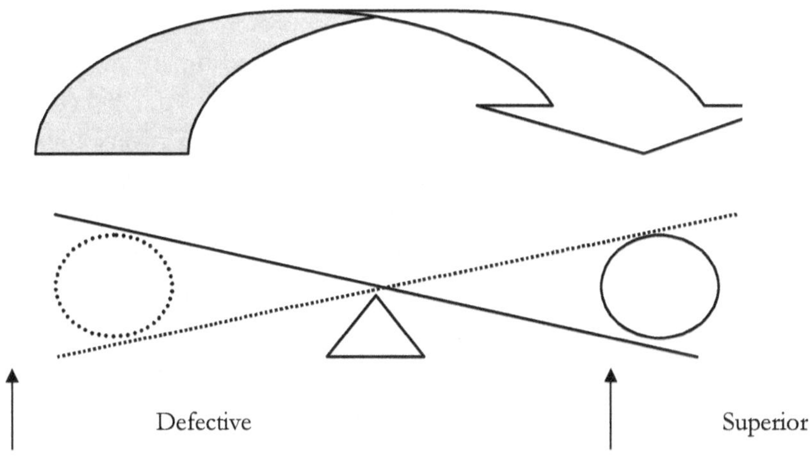

The core belief of "I am defective" has an underlying feeling of shame. On one end of the seesaw, the person feels the shame and will look insecure and without confidence. The person who surrenders or "gives in" to his defectiveness core belief thinks, feels, and acts as he was defective. On the other end of the seesaw, the person counterattacks his feeling of shame and tries to see himself as special and superior. However, one mistake and he will flip to the defective side. He constantly has to reassure himself and others that he is the "top dog." If others criticize him, "disrespect" him or somehow suggest that he is not superior, then he might flip to the other side of the seesaw and feel the shame of his defectiveness. Thus staying on the superior side is a strain and constant struggle.

Both ends of the all-or-nothing defectiveness seesaw of either feeling superior or defective are extreme and self-destructive.

Balanced Alternatives to the Defectiveness Core Belief

Being an individual, loving and trusting yourself—these are the balanced beliefs needed to counter the abandonment all-or-nothing seesaws. The same theme of self-love also heals the defectiveness life trap and provides a balance for this all-or-nothing seesaw.

Accepting yourself as a worthwhile person may be difficult, especially if you have act behaved in violent and hurtful ways. You feel shame for these past actions, which reinforces your belief that you are an unlovable person. You have not acted in a very lovable way, and your behaviors may have pushed people away, so in fact, at this moment, not many people may love you.

You need to separate your *behaviors* from your *worth* as a person. You should feel guilt about your behaviors but no shame for who you are. You are a fallible human being—a person who makes mistakes but still is worth something. To help you accept this, try to remember yourself before you began acting in unpleasant or hurtful ways. Go back to yourself as an infant or small child who just wanted to be loved. This child was you and was special and precious.

Acceptance of one's self as a person who can make mistakes but who can change for the better is a healthy and balanced alternative for the defectiveness all-or-nothing seesaw.

Defectiveness All-or-Nothing Seesaw with Balanced Middle

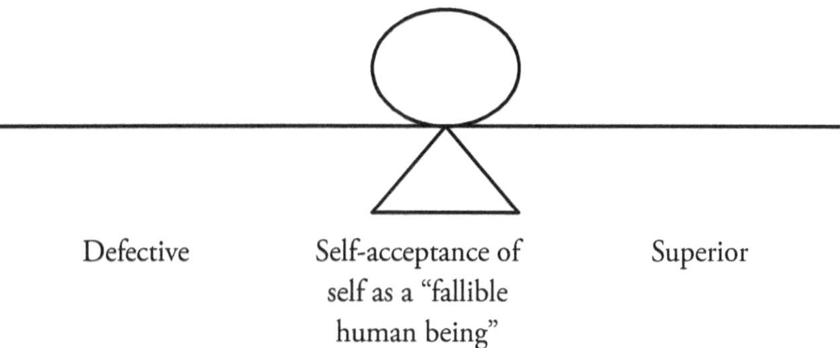

Mistrust/Abuse "All-or-Nothing" Seesaw

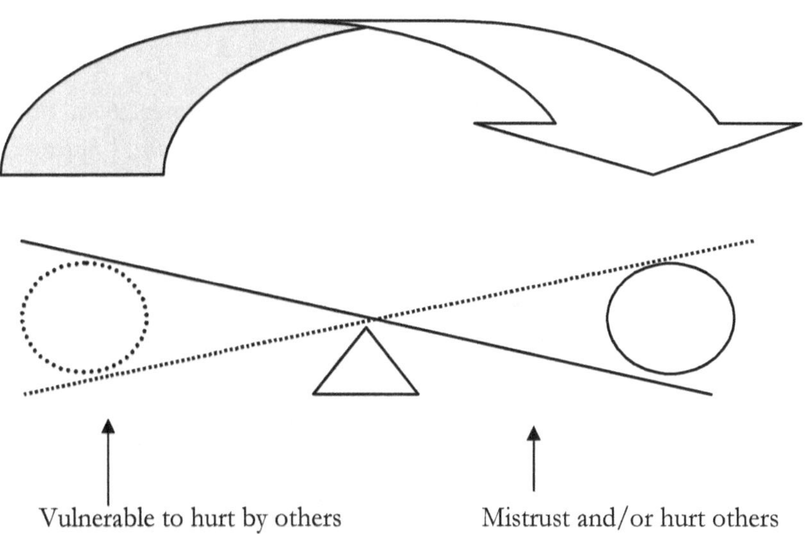

On the one end of the mistrust/abuse seesaw, the person feels hurt by others or vulnerable to hurt. He trusts too much. To avoid being vulnerable or hurt, they flip to the other side and mistrust others or even try to hurt others first. The anger and hurt from the one extreme of the seesaw generalizes to everyone and they are quick to attack other people because they expect these other people to hurt them.

Some people try to stay on the left side and try to trust others. They want to trust so badly that they will ignore signs that this person is not trustworthy. They'll just go along and hope this time, this person will not hurt them. Or else they feel comfortable being hurt. Although it is painful, the hurt is familiar.

Balanced Beliefs for the Mistrust/Abuse Life Trap

It is difficult for people who have been hurt in the past to learn to trust again. Some try to trust others again and keep getting hurt. Let's look at the idea of trusting others and what it means to be "emotionally hurt" by others.

As a child, you needed adults to take care of you. A child is dependent on the good will of adults for both his material and emotional needs. A child left alone might easily die and a child not given love will not be able to develop a healthy sense of himself or the world. A child has many emotional needs.

However, what is true about an adult's "needs?" This author believes the theory of psychologist Albert Ellis that adults *need* only air, food, water, and warmth. Let's look at the alcoholic who swears, "I need a drink (of alcohol)." Does he really need alcohol? No, of course not. Yet by claiming that alcohol is a need, he is overwhelmed by a feeling of need. With this thought, it is very difficult to stop himself from drinking alcohol. If it were true that he really needed the drink of alcohol, he would die without it. A more reasonable way for him to think is "I'd like a drink, but I do not need it." Thinking this way helps this person gain some objectivity and feel more in control. It becomes easier to make the behavioral choice of whether to get some alcohol or not. This is another example of "How we think determines how we act."

Do we as adult human beings need others to provide nurturance, comfort, and support? There have in fact been various examples of individuals who have survived without love, comfort, and support. Their lives may not have been emotionally healthy or particularly joyful but they did indeed survive. How can we survive without love from others? We survive by giving love to ourselves. We survive by learning to feel good about ourselves when we set a goal and achieve it. We feel good about ourselves when we draw or create a poem, when we pray to a spiritual being, or when we walk outside in nature.

By learning to provide for some of our own emotional needs, we become less dependent on other people. We can avoid rushing into relationships with the first person that comes along and can be somewhat picky in whom we choose to be with. We can wait and choose a person worthy of our love and trust.

Can other people be trusted? When you have always seen yourself as needing other people, you may have jumped into relationships with people who were indeed not very worthy of trust. Why weren't these people worthy of trust? They were not trustworthy because they had their own life traps. Remember, a person with life traps does not make good choices about their feelings or behaviors. They may love you but still act in ways that hurt you and/or hurt the relationship. Their own distorted core beliefs and life traps may lead them to make choices that hurt you. They may be wonderful people who are worthy of love, but they cannot be trusted to always make good behavioral choices. Their actions mean nothing about your self-worth.

Others cannot hurt you when you have good *boundaries*. You can let others in or zip up your shield and protect yourself. You can set limits and let others know how you want to be treated. If others don't respect your boundaries, you can choose to leave the relationship.

No matter how loving and trustworthy another person may be, only you can make choices for you. You are the person you need to love and trust and depend on. If you love and trust yourself, no one can hurt you emotionally. *You can provide your own emotional needs by loving yourself.*

Mistrust/Abuse All-or-Nothing Seesaw with Balanced Middle

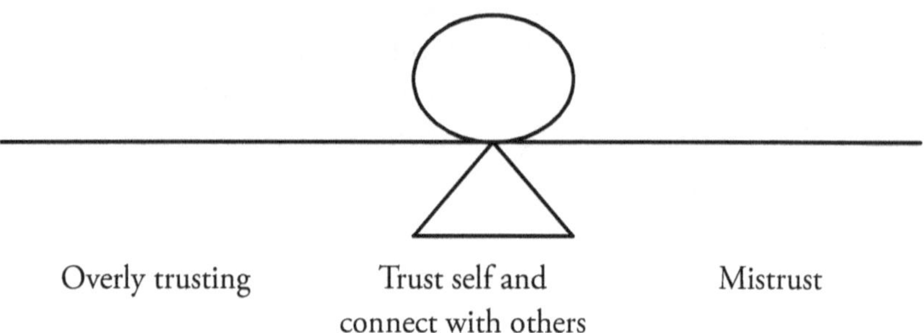

Emotional Deprivation "All-or-Nothing" Seesaw

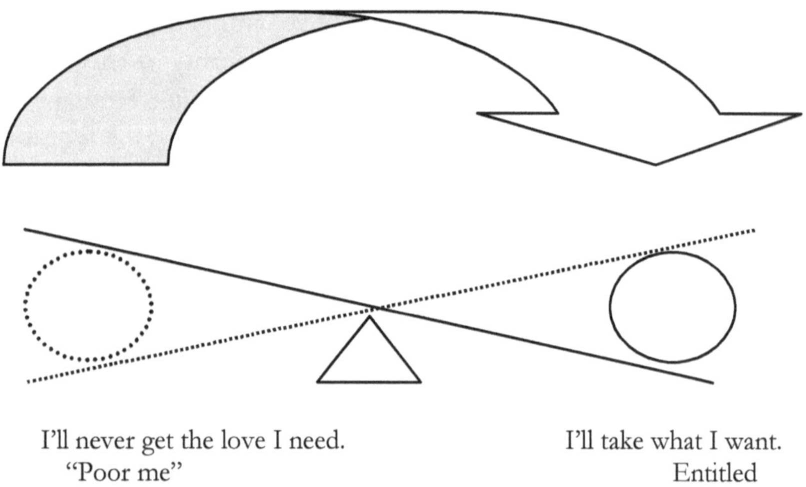

At the one end, the person believes that he will never get the love he needs. He feels sorry for himself and is full of self-pity. He feels empty inside like he is never going to get what he feels he needs. He might "give up" and figure "Nothing matters anymore." This feeling can lead to violence and self-defeating behavior because "It doesn't matter what I do."

At the other end of the emotional deprivation seesaw, the person decides that not only should he get the love he needs, he should get everything he wants and thinks he needs. He's going to get it for himself if others don't give it to him. With all-or-nothing thinking, the person interprets any one thing that he does not get as a sign that he will not get anything he wants or needs. He will never get anything that he wants or needs and he will be deprived forever.

Entitlement involves the irrational belief described below by psychologist Albert Ellis:

> The world (and the people in it) must arrange conditions so that I get everything I want when I want it. Also conditions must exist that I don't get what I don't want. Furthermore, I must get what I want quickly and easily.

The logic implicit in this belief is that because you do not personally like something or don't want something to happen, or if you find someone's behavior undesirable or even obnoxious, then it *should not* happen or that person *must not* behave that way. This demand that the world act the way that we think it should is part of "entitlement."

Emotional Deprivation Seesaw with Balanced Middle

You can probably guess the alternative belief to the emotional deprivation all-or-nothing seesaw. That's right. You can give yourself the love and caring you need. Try the inner child visualization. Tell yourself what you wanted to hear as a child. Treat yourself as you would treat your own best friend.

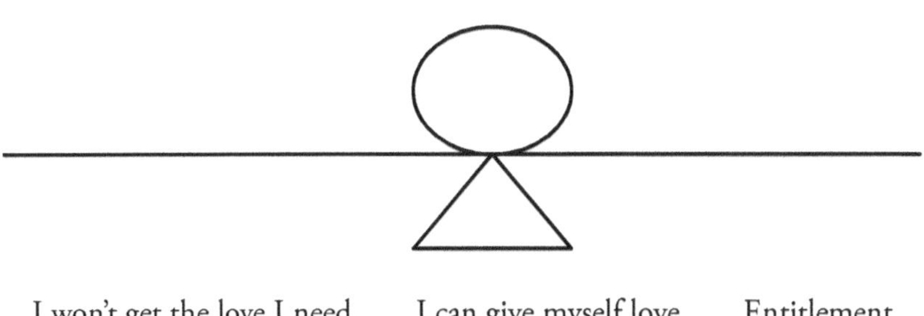

Powerlessness "All-or-Nothing" Seesaw

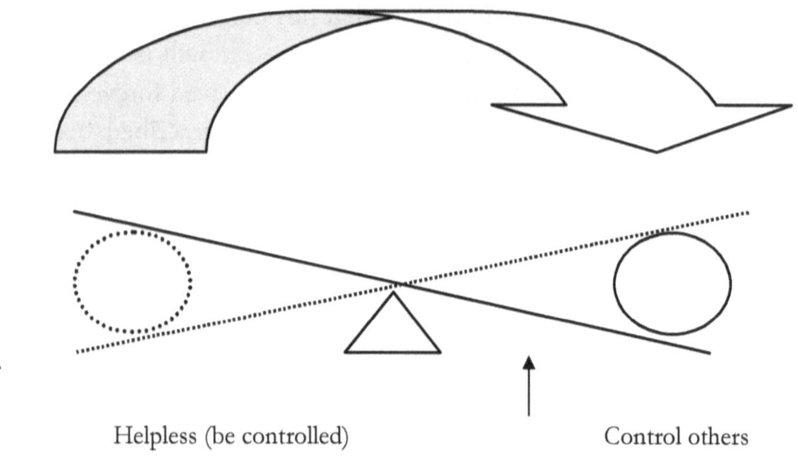

On the powerlessness seesaw, the core belief is that one is helpless and controlled by others. In all-or-nothing thinking, one is either in control or totally controlled. The world is a power struggle. Surrendering to this belief, the person gives up his needs and desires to others who are believed to have control over him.

To reject this belief and its feelings of helplessness, the person flips to the other side of the seesaw and tries to control others. He believes that he can control others and his world and by being controlling, he can avoid feeling powerless. If things go his way, he feels powerful. However, when things don't go his way, he feels out-of-control and angry. Every frustration, every time his desires are not met means that he is *not in control and powerless*. He counterattacks by trying to control others. When he believes that he gets someone else to do what he wants, he feels more or at least temporally less powerless. This gives at least a temporary sense of satisfaction and pleasure.

Balanced Beliefs about Power and Control

Some things we have little or no control over. We cannot control the weather. We cannot prevent tornadoes or earthquakes. We can't change the day we were born or change the life we have lived up until this point in time. We cannot always prevent or keep cancer or other terminal illnesses from hurting our loved ones or ourselves.

We are able to control to some degree things like our health; for example, we can eat a balanced diet, exercise, and get adequate rest. We can control, to some degree, the safety of our adult homes and our community by working with our neighbors, supporting the police, and getting involved in local government. We are able to "influence" others to do what we would like them to do by telling them what we would like, trying to convince them that "our way" is right and by setting limits and consequences if they abuse us. For example, you might tell your partner that you will leave a relationship if that person continues to drink, has sex with others, or is violent.

However, no matter how healthy of a lifestyle we try to live, we still can get a terminal illness or get in an accident that hurts our health. No matter how much we try to protect our families, there are still people who choose to steal and hurt others. No matter how much we threaten, loved ones may still choose to drink or be violent. No one can control you totally and you cannot control the world.

It is true that as a child, you were relatively helpless and out of control of your life. However, this is not true now. You can control your own thoughts, feelings, and behaviors as well as influence a good portion of the circumstances of your own life. Even in prison or on supervision, you have control over if and when you choose to follow the rules; you have choices about your attitude and your feelings about the rules.

For those of you who counterattack and try to control others: *You do not run the universe. Things do not have to go your way.*

Reality is reality, not the way you'd like it to be. People act in ways that we don't like, they make their choices about their behaviors and do what they think is the right thing to do at the time. If everyone always followed rules and laws, we wouldn't need a prison.

Sometimes others choose to disrespect others, sometimes life isn't fair, and sometimes you don't always get what you want or what you thought you needed. We can give negative consequences after behaviors we don't like, but we cannot control the others' decision to act. We need to learn to accept reality as it is, not the way we'd like it to be.

It helps to accept reality by putting it into two categories:

1.   Things you can change.
2.   Things you can't change.

You cannot directly change other people's behavior. They make their own choices. You can change your own reaction to others and events. You are in control of your own thoughts, feelings, attitudes, and behaviors.

The Serenity Prayer

Grant me that serenity to accept the things I cannot change.
The strength to change the things I can.
And the wisdom to know the difference.
(Anonymous)

Powerlessness All-or-Nothing Seesaw with Balanced Middle

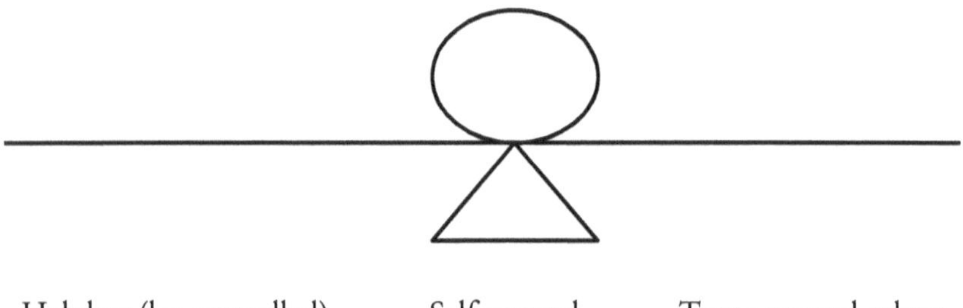

Helpless (be controlled)   Self-control   Try to control others

Summary on "Getting off the All-or-Nothing Seesaw and Healing your Life Traps"

While the core beliefs made some sense when you were a child, *they do not make sense now.*

When you were a child and all of the adults around you were telling you that there was something wrong with you, it made sense to begin to believe that you were somehow defective. However, just because the adults gave you a message that you were defective and it made sense to believe it then, does not mean it is *true*. The adults in your world as a child had their own life traps. They had their own problems, and the fact that they did not give you the love you needed does not mean you are unlovable.

Because maladaptive core beliefs were developed when we were children when we thought in primitive, immature, and illogical ways, the core beliefs and thinking involved in a life trap is often illogical and doesn't make a whole lot of sense. However, because there is so much emotion associated with our life traps, it is difficult to simply "think them away." Difficult does not mean that it's not worth doing. Thus to get off the "all-or-nothing" seesaws, we need to challenge our core beliefs and develop alternative, balanced beliefs about others, the world, and ourselves.

ANNOTATED BIBLIOGRAPHY

Allen, J.G. *Coping with Trauma: A Guide to Self-Understanding.* Washington, DC: American Psychiatric Press, 1995.
An in-depth self-help book discussing the effects of trauma.

Athens, L. H. *The Creation of Dangerous Violent Criminals.* Illinois: University of Chicago Press, 1992.
Criminologist interviews brutal and hardened violent criminals. Shows how criminals undergo a tortuous learning process and experiences leading them to malevolence.

Bateman, A. W. and P. Fonagy. *Handbook of Mentalizing in Mental Health Practice.* Washington, DC: American Psychiatric Publishing, Inc., 2012.
Written for clinician, outlines the development of social cognition in humans. Fascinating for understanding pre-logical thinking processes characteristic of psychiatric disorders.

Baumeister, R. F. *Meanings of Life.* Guilford Press: New York, 1991.
Answers to the question "What is the meaning of life?" Beautifully written.

Blum, D. *Love at Goon Park: Harry Harlow and the Science of Affection.* Perseus Publishing, 2002.
Very informative, easy to read, and important for understanding the human need for love.

Course of Miracles. 1976. http://en.wikipedia.org.
A book containing a curriculum which claims to assist readers in a spiritual transformation. Forms the foundation for the books by Dr. Lee Jampolsky and Robin Casarjian.

Curtois, C. A. *It's Not You, It's What Happened to You: Complex Trauma and Treatment.* Telemachus Press, 2014.

An excellent, easy to read review of Complex-PTSD.

Dutton, D. G. *The Abusive Personality: Violence and Control in Intimate Relationships.* New York: Guilford Press, 1998.

Dutton had a more recent book, but I believe this one best discusses the psychology of domestically violent men.

Ellis, A. *Better, Deeper, and More Enduring Brief Therapy: The Rational Emotive Behavior Therapy Approach.* Brunner/Mazel: New York, 1996.

Fromm, E. *The Art of Loving.* Harper and Row: New York, 1956. Brilliant but difficult treatise on the nature of love.

Gilligan, J. *Violence: Reflections on a National Epidemic.* New York: Vintage Books, 1996.

Very important discussion on the causes of violence and recommendations for society on how to confront it. Written by a Harvard psychiatrist who was director of mental health for the Massachusetts prison system.

Goleman, D. *Emotional Intelligence: Why It Can Matter More Than IQ.* New York: Bantam Books, 1995.

A classic everyone should read.

Hotchkiss, S. *Why Is It Always About You? The Seven Deadly Sins of Narcissism.* New York: Free Press, 2003.

A popular book about traits of narcissism.

Jampolsky, L. *Healing the Addictive Personality.* New York: Random House, Inc., 2008.

Excellent self-help book explaining the beliefs underlying the addictive personality.

Kushner, H. S. *When Children Ask about God.* New York: Schocken Books, 1971.

The rabbi (author of *When Bad Things Happen to Good People)* explains basic tenants in the Jewish religion.

Layden, M. A., et al. *Cognitive Therapy of Borderline Personality Disorder.* Boston: Allyn and Bacon, 1993.

Chapter two, "Developmental Issues of Borderline Personality Disorder," addresses Eriksonian and Piagetian development stages with childhood trauma.

Levine, A. and R. S. F. Heller. *Attached: The New Science of Adult Attachment and How It Can Help You Find—and Keep—Love.* New York: Penguin Press, 2010.
Self-help book; very informative.

Lewis, M. (*Shame: The Exposed Self.* New York: The Free Press, 1992. Starting with the story of Adam and Eve, Dr. Lewis explores this emotion of self-consciousness and its importance in psychology.

Moskowitz, A. "Dissociation and Violence: A Review of the Literature." *Trauma, Violence, & Abuse,* vol. 5 no. 1, January 21–46. 2008.
An excellent review.

Muller, R. T. *Trauma and the Avoidant Client: Attachment-Based Strategies for Healing.* New York: W. W. Norton, 2010. A book for mental health clinicians.

Nauth, L. N. *Lifetraps: A Workbook for Understanding and Change.* The Wisconsin Department of Corrections, 2011.

Perry, B. D. *Violence and Childhood: Understanding Traumatized and Maltreated Children: The Core Concepts.* www.ChildTrauma. org. 2004.

Shaw, D. *Traumatic Narcissism: Relational Systems of Subjugation.* New York: Routledge, 2014.
Based on psychoanalytical theory and very difficult to read.

Siegel, D. J. *The Developing Mind: How Relationships and the Brain Interact to Shape Who We Are.* New York: Guilford Press, 2012.
One of my favorite resources in helping me understand the neuroscience of memory, attachment, and states of mind.

Stosny, S. *Treating Attachment Abuse: A Compassionate Approach.* New York: Springer, 1995.
Important reading for anyone in the field of domestic violence.

Van Der Kolk, B. *The Body Keeps the Score: Brain, Mind, and Body in the Healing of Trauma.* New York: Viking, 2014.
Interesting for mental health practitioners and/or victims regarding the mind-body connection based on thirty years of research and clinical work by a leader in trauma research.

Wallen, D. J. *Attachment in Psychotherapy.* New York: Guilford Press, 2007. Good application of attachment to therapy.

Young, J. E. and Klosko, J. S. *Reinventing Your Life: How to Break Free from Negative Life Patterns and Feel Good Again.* New York: Plume, 1994.
I don't know anyone who read this book and did not find some insight about self-defeating life patterns.

Young, J. E., J. S. Klosko, and M. E. Weishaar. *Schema Therapy: A Practitioner's Guide.* New York: Guilford Press, 2003.
The first half of the book describes schemas; the second half concerns modes which I have not found helpful.

Ziggler, D. *Traumatic Experience and the Brain: A Hand Book for Understanding and Treating Those Traumatized as Children.* Phoenix, AZ: Acacia Press, 2002.
Excellent and a must-read.